SPLENDID ICE CREAM
DESSERTS

SPLENDID ICE CREAM
DESSERTS

Jeni Britton Bauer

ARTISAN

NEW YORK

Published by Artisan
A division of Workman Publishing Company, Inc.
225 Varick Street
New York, NY 10014-4381
artisanbooks.com

Published simultaneously in Canada by Thomas Allen & Son, Limited.

Library of Congress Cataloging-in-Publication Data

Bauer, Jeni Britton.
Jeni's splendid ice cream desserts / Jeni Britton Bauer.
pages cm
Includes index.
ISBN 978-1-57965-592-1
1. Ice cream, ices, etc. 2. Frozen desserts. I. Title.
TX795.B383 2014
641.86'2—dc23   2013042228

Design by Renata Di Biase
Photographs by Kelsey McClellan

Printed in Canada
First printing, April 2014

10 9 8 7 6 5 4 3 2 1

CONTENTS

A PROMISE

Ice cream desserts are like my favorite people—they look the best when they are starting to fall apart. Not sloppy, but confidently disheveled, like the late great Paul Newman stepping out of his race car, or Diane Keaton in *Annie Hall,* or Tatum O'Neal in *Paper Moon.* Ice cream desserts have personality to spare. Sweetened cream slowly dripping from a frozen scoop transforms a cake or sauce the moment it touches it. Butterfat-rich cream absorbs scent and flavor and carries them to your nose. Anything ice cream touches becomes richer, more flavorful, more deeply perceived.

What's more, ice cream encourages you to be in the moment. It's melting and changing each second—you have to pay attention to it, or it disappears.

In these pages you will find a few solid recipes that you will use over and over again and tweak with the season, the menu, or your whim. Each cake, pie, fritter, ice cream, sauce, and sundae is phenomenal in flavor and texture, and each recipe is designed specifically for the home kitchen. While I won't declare that every recipe in this book is fast and easy (even though many are), I will say they are as streamlined as we can make them and the results are truly worth the effort. You can dress them up or down, depending on how you plate them or which ice cream you serve with them.

When was the last time you had a Bette? Apple Bette is one of the finest recipes to serve with ice cream and my recipe calls for croissants or brioche that turn into a wonderful buttery fruit bread pudding. I also give you my recipe for Fruit Crisp because it's darn good. It's a little crispier than others and there's too much streusel (that is, just enough). Then there are cobblers, and mine have extra fruit and creamy-as-heck biscuits plopped in. Like everything in this book, they're all tailor-made for a scoop of ice cream.

The ice creams that you will make from this book are as delicious as those we make in our professional kitchens—utterly creamy and scoopable, with layers of flavor—or I wouldn't put my name on it. New ones abound, including our Crème sans Lait (a vegan option that will knock your socks off), a rich and tasty frozen custard, and a soft-serve. The gooey sauces are as versatile as everything else we do and can be made with a variety of spices, salts, or herbs. Choose a cake, pie, or poached fruit from Bakeshop, pair it with an ice cream from Ice Cream Parlor, and top with a sauce from The Basics, and you've got a dessert that can accompany any meal or mood.

We have made and eaten these recipes over and over and are positively thrilled with the results. I hope that you will dive into this book and make it yours. Drip, drizzle, and mark up the pages at will! There is no better compliment in the world than a battered and beaten-up book.

To more pleasures!
Jeni

FLAVORS THAT BLOOM

Before I started making ice cream, I studied art at The Ohio State University, worked in a bakery, and had a serious hobby blending perfumes and collecting rare essential oils. Though I didn't know it at the time, that could not have been a more perfect foundation for a would-be ice cream maker. I draw daily from what I learned in each of these areas. Ice cream is where food, art, perfume, and science collide.

Food

I'm proud that we make our ice creams and everything that goes into them in our kitchens in Columbus, not in factories. Our kitchens look like those of bustling restaurants at high noon. We don't use "dump and freeze" ingredients like mixes, pastes, flavorings, and colorings. We find really tasty ingredients from all over the world that we cook, peel, bake, boil, fry, ladle, and/or crumble into ice creams. You will use the same techniques in this book that we do in our kitchens, and they all begin with *food*.

Imagine if you found out that all craft brewers made beer from an off-the-shelf beer mix and just added a couple of drops of flavoring to it before bottling it under their "craft beer" label. When I first started making ice creams, I assumed that an ice cream kitchen would look like any busy bakery or pastry kitchen, that cooks and chefs would be at their stations in white aprons making ice cream. It's not true. Most so-called artisan, homemade, or craft ice creams are made with purchased liquid or powdered ice cream mixes and added flavorings and colorings. Anybody can add flavorings to a mix. To actually craft an ice cream from scratch is to choose ingredients at their peak and understand how to use them at

the precise moment to make their flavors shine brightest. And that's what we do at Jeni's.

Art

I am not an artist, but I could not make ice cream the way I do without a foundation of art. Art guides how I think about ice cream, and the methods I learned while studying art often guide me in business as well. Art is not just aesthetic. What you take out is as important as what you put in. What you don't say is as important as what you do.

To make ice creams that are aesthetically pleasing, that have a bright, clear, compelling flavor profile, you have to put some thought into it. Art, you could say, answers the question "Why?" Why make this or that ice cream? Why add color, or not? Why use natural color? Why bergamot? Why chamomile? Why lemon? Why is crunch right for this flavor?

Could I make an ice cream inspired by a 1973 lemon-yellow Camaro? Heck, yes. The car makes my heart go pitter-patter, and I know that Lemon Yellow Camaro Ice Cream would too. It would go like this: tart, lemony cream steeped with chamomile, with crushed acidic bergamot hard candy strewn throughout. The ice cream would be a crisp, creamy white, the candy would have a milk-glass-citron look. Lemon tastes like the color yellow. The candy looks and feels like the car's shiny lacquer-like finish. The chamomile provides a slight scent of summer wildflowers, apples, and hay—the fragrance of Ohio summer air.

But it's not literally about the car. When you can answer the whys to everything you make or do, the details build up to become the experience. That's the art.

Perfume

For a while in the mid-1990s, I thought about becoming a professional perfumer, aka a nose. I'd been dabbling in blending essential oils into perfumes. I loved it so much that I resolved, when I could afford it, to run away to Grasse, France, and become a professional nose. Which, I suppose, was a little like saying you are going to Monte Carlo to become a race car driver. I actually had no idea how to break into the business, or where exactly to go once I got to Grasse, and I had no money anyway. But that became my plan. . . . And then I found ice cream.

Ice cream is edible perfume. As the frozen cream melts on your tongue, it carries flavor to your nose—the flavor it is composed of and the flavor of what it is resting on. Butterfat (the fat in milk and cream) is special: it absorbs scent and melts just below body temperature. You can bury layers of scent in ice cream, top, middle, and base notes, all of varying degrees of strength. It's the same as when ancient perfumers layered precious scents in oils and fats that, when applied, were volatized by the warmth of the person's skin into the air around them. Perfumers choose a carrier because of how it melts or evaporates on the skin. If an oil is too heavy, the scent will not be released. Butterfat melts at just below body temperature, at 95°F, making it an excellent carrier for scent.

Your olfactory system has the remarkable ability to transport you through space and time.

You've no doubt experienced this. Whenever, for instance, I eat fresh scallions, I am transported back to my grandmother's garden, where we would eat just-picked scallions raw. I can't eat one now without feeling as if I am seven years old again and standing at her side in the garden.

Sweetened cream is a blank canvas upon which to build a scentful composition that will transport your guests to other places in time or space—through their noses! Whether you travel to Vietnam and bring back fragrant cinnamon, find the most luscious peaches on a small farm in Georgia, or harvest mint from your own backyard, ice cream is the perfect way to tell your stories. You will be swept away, right along with your guests. Such is the power of scent.

Science

My lifelong pursuit has been achieving a specific buttercream texture in our ice creams. That ultrasmooth, almost chewy, cleanly melting ice cream first lived mostly in my imagination, but now, increasingly, it's in the pints of ice cream that we create in our kitchens. Still, I go to work each day thinking I will make better ice cream today than I did the day before, and I will make better ice cream the next day than I do today. Our ice cream has indeed gotten better and better over the years, and, what's more, we've changed how ice cream can be made, both on a commercial level and in a home kitchen. This aspect of ice cream making is thrilling because it is based on active learning, trying, tweaking, and growing—science.

As I explained in more detail in my first book, *Jeni's Splendid Ice Creams at Home,* the balance of ingredients determines the balance of the sensory facets of an ice cream: flavor, texture, body, and finish. Everything you add to an ice cream will affect the finished product. It will make it smoother or icier, denser or fluffier, spongier or lighter, elastic or crumbly, and so on. When I started making ice cream, I was still doing my best to avoid math and science in my life. I now play for both teams, art and science. If you want to create a beautiful ice cream, you must have the soul of an artist but think like a scientist.

This book is about my way of making ice cream and what I like to serve with it. Other ice cream makers have their preferences as to how to combine ingredients and deal with the trade-offs that come with those decisions. And you will have yours. It's all drop-dead delightful—and it's all science.

IN THIS BOOK

In this book, I share my favorite desserts served over the years in our scoop shops, along with desserts our team enjoys during our company lunches and those I make for guests at home. The lineup includes cakes, pies, fritters, sauces, and much more. The recipes are low-fuss, big-bang, and very versatile. For example, Sweet Empanadas (page 140) can be made with almost any fruit. I like to squash them on the plate and drop ice cream right on top. The steam billows out, and the ice cream slowly melts into a sauce. If you carefully choose the ice cream and the fruit, you can determine the emotion of the dessert at your table.

Cakes exemplify how various compositions can be created using elements from different parts of this book. For instance, cake plus ice cream plus sauce plus garnishes—all stacked together in a silicone springform mold—make for a superlative ice cream layer cake (see pages 170–75). If you're a chocolate lover, layer the whole thing with chocolate cake, chocolate sauce, chocolate ice cream, and even Chocolate Gravel (page 196)—each slice drips and beckons. Want something more colorful and fruity? Use the Lady Cake (page 100) and add a colorful frozen yogurt, a fruit sauce, and fresh berries—it's perfect on a Sunday afternoon with pink Champagne.

There are three main chapters in this book: Ice Cream Parlor, Bakeshop, and Sundae Bar. In Ice Cream Parlor, you will find our brand-new recipes, including Salty Vanilla Frozen Custard, Buttermilk Soft-Serve, and even an amazing dairy-free option, our Crème sans Lait. Bakeshop offers Stone-Ground-Grits Pudding Cake, Bauer House Biscuits, and more one-of-a-kind baked goodies, as well as Peoria Corn Fritters, an Apple Rhubarb Bette, and other tasty desserts to accompany ice creams. And Sundae Bar is chock-full of cocktails, sundae combinations, and plated desserts combining different elements from the other chapters.

Following these chapters is The Basics, which provides recipes that can be used in multiple ways in other recipes throughout the book—gravels, sauces, jams, glazes, and more.

About the Recipes

For my first book, *Jeni's Splendid Ice Creams at Home,* I set myself the challenge of developing recipes that produce the same taste, texture, body, and finish as those we make in our professional kitchens, using ingredients and equipment readily available to a home cook. The goal was to make ice creams indistinguishable from the Jeni's scoop shop ice creams, and we succeeded. The project involved a retooling of every step of the ice-cream-making process, which is why my recipes are unique. People throughout the world now use my recipes to make ice creams for their friends and family. Ice cream businesses using my recipes have popped up across the country, from San Francisco to

Brooklyn, and people from South Africa to Indonesia have been inspired by my recipes, techniques, and flavors.

The new recipes in this, my second book, are made on the same model, but they have been slightly updated to address changes in ice cream machines. Among the new machines, there's the ice cream bowl attachment for the Breville mixer, which we love, and a new version of the Cuisinart 1½-quart canister machine, which is faster at freezing ice cream than the previous model. In fact, the newest Cuisinart freezes ice cream so fast that the body of the ice cream never has time to expand, and it comes out too compact. So, I've adjusted my recipes to accommodate for that and to work well in the various Breville machines.

Although I am known for creating flavors that are all over the map, from sweet to savory, old school to new school, ancient to modern, the most important innovations in my ice cream recipes center on achieving that scoopable buttercream consistency. Once you master these recipes, you can create any flavor your heart desires. If you have an idea, try it—if it works, put your name on it. That's what I've done for the last twenty years! It's what makes ice cream so much fun.

My hope is that the recipes for the new ice creams and desserts in this book will serve as a jumping-off point for all the wonderful flavors you are dying to make—and that making ice creams and other desserts will bring you, your friends, and your family as much delight as it has to ours.

INTOLERANTS

If you are holding this book, chances are good you are a dairy and gluten eater. But chances are also very good that you know someone who, for whatever reason, does not eat either of these. It's nice to have options that work for everyone—that way, one of your guests isn't stuck with a pile of grapes for dessert while the rest of your table indulges in ice cream and cake. When you are hosting people, it is your job to make them feel

good, so having a few reliable dairy-free, vegan, and/or gluten-free dessert options is a must. I have created recipes for my friends and relatives who live vegan or gluten or dairy free—and for their friends. But these are not recipes just for people who can't have what most of us can—they are desserts for everyone. Throughout this book, when a recipe is naturally gluten free or works well made with gluten-free flour, you will see this symbol: **G**.

When a recipe is dairy free, it will have this symbol: **D**, and if it is vegan, it will have this: **V**.

The Ice Cream Tool Kit

There are recipes for three different types of ice cream in this book, plus recipes for frozen yogurts and sorbets.

SWEET CREAM ICE CREAM

My classic, creamy, smooth ice cream base (see page 28) is slightly chewy and elastic enough to roll into a proper ice cream ball when scooped. It's low in air and the ideal blank canvas, but it is not without flavor. It is excellent on its own as a simple sweet cream or when swirled with a sauce or jam. I have updated the recipe slightly from my first book, partly to accommodate new machines that are available but also just to make it slightly better. The changes are not huge, however, so keep in mind that the older recipes and the new ones in this book all work wonderfully in whichever machine you own.

FROZEN CUSTARD

Frozen custard is ice cream made with egg yolks. My recipe for frozen custard is smooth and creamy, supple and scoopable, and it has a distinctive rich flavor and extra chewiness from the egg yolks. This is not the soft-serve frozen custard variety found throughout the Midwest; it is American scoop-shop custard, meant to be served hard. But you can serve it however you'd like—right out of the machine, when it is still soft, or after it hardens. I give you a base recipe (see page 60) so that you can use it to make other varieties as well.

CRÈME SANS LAIT

I call my dairy-free ice cream Crème sans Lait, because it is so delicious that it deserves a place in every kitchen—and its own fancy name. Our Crème sans Lait is every bit "Jeni's" in taste, texture, body, and finish. It is dense and übercreamy, with a lovely rich flavor. You can roll it into a scoop and perch it atop a cone to be licked slowly on a hot August day. It's not only for your intolerant pals, it's for you, too. We love it. Pair it with Brrrr Sauce (page 186) for one of the most yummy ice cream desserts you've ever had, vegan or not.

SOFT-SERVE ICE CREAM

Although they are a little gimmicky, I love the new at-home soft-serve machines. We use ours to make a light, fun buttermilk soft-serve. You can make it into any flavor, but I like it best just plain and used in a sundae or served with Peoria Corn Fritters (page 136). The recipe can be used in any ice cream machine, not just soft-serve models—just serve it immediately, as soon as it is done. Of course, you can also harden it in the freezer and serve it that way. The base recipe (see page 68) can be made with whole or 2% milk, but buttermilk gives this ice cream the most exciting burst of flavor.

YOGURTS

Every chef who has ever had our yogurts declares ours to be her or his favorite (I won't name-drop, but consider these people among the finest chefs in the world). I am trying to go overboard on praise here, because you may think that frozen yogurts are "health food" and I want you to think of them as purely delicious. Serve them with all of your desserts! These yogurts are creamy, light, tart, and refreshing. They work best in fruit flavors, and tart fruit works best because it reflects the tartness of the yogurt; nevertheless, sweeter fruits, like mango, also work scrumptiously.

SORBETS

Sorbets are composed of sugar syrup, fruit, and, occasionally, a liquor. They're frozen in an ice cream machine like ice cream. The trick with sorbet is to get just the right balance to make it scoopable but not too soupy. All sorbets will be very light and even a tad icy, but their charm is in the pop of flavor that they add to any dessert.

THE QUICK TAKE

Here is an overview of the process of making ice cream. In general, there are four basic steps: Prep, Cook, Chill, and Freeze. However, each ice cream is different, so be sure to read the individual recipe's directions fully before beginning.

THE STEPS

ADVANCE PREP

Some ice creams have an extra, preliminary step, called Advance Prep, which often should be done the day before. This can be anything from straining yogurt or toasting nuts to making a sauce or a cake.

Frozen yogurts always require the advance step of straining the yogurt. To do so, secure a mesh sieve over a bowl and place two layers of cheesecloth over the sieve. Pour 1 quart of plain lowfat yogurt over the cheesecloth into the sieve, and put the bowl in the refrigerator for 6 to 8 hours. Discard the strained liquid and use the concentrated yogurt to make your frozen yogurt.

PREP Gather all tools and equipment so they are close at hand. Measure out all ingredients so that they are ready to go when the moment calls. Then in a small bowl, make a slurry with the cornstarch and 2 tablespoons of milk. In a medium bowl, whip all the lumps out of the room-temperature cream cheese (and egg yolks, if making a custard). And finally, in a large bowl, set up an ice bath (with extra ice) and keep it ready for the Chill step.

COOK Pour the milk, cream, sugar, and corn syrup into a 4-quart saucepan and bring to a boil. When bubbles become regular, set a timer for exactly 4 minutes—the timing is important. Turn off the heat and slowly pour in the cornstarch slurry, in a steady stream, stirring constantly. Return to a boil and keep stirring for about 30 seconds until slightly thickened.

CHILL Slowly pour the hot cream mixture into the cream cheese, a little at a time, incorporating each pour fully before adding more. Pour the hot ice cream base into a Ziploc bag, push all air out, and seal. Submerge completely in the ice bath and leave there until very cold, at least 30 minutes.

FREEZE When the base is completely cool and you are ready to freeze the ice cream, assemble the ice cream machine and turn it on. Remove the ice cream base from the ice bath and cut a corner off the bag. Pour the base into the center of the machine. When the ice cream is thick and creamy and it's beginning to rise out of the machine, turn the motor off. Remove the lid and dasher and transfer the ice cream to a storage container. Cover the surface with parchment and freeze until firm, about 4 hours.

LUSCIOUS
GRASS-GRAZED
CREAM
EXQUISITE
INGREDIENTS
BUILT FROM
THE
GROUND UP

THE ICE CREAM SYSTEM

My ice cream recipe system has four steps: Prep, Cook, Chill, and Freeze. Occasionally a recipe contains an Advance Prep step, which must be completed before you start the ice-cream-making process.

ADVANCE PREP

Advance Prep covers everything you need to do before you start making your ice cream, frozen yogurt, or sorbet. If an ice cream contains a fruit sauce or mix-in, you need to prepare it before you begin. All of my frozen yogurts require straining the yogurt, which must be done at least 6 hours in advance. When a recipe has an Advance Prep step, you'll need to budget a bit more time.

PREP

Prepping is about your *mise en place,* your setup. It means measuring everything out and getting everything ready to go so that it is there the moment you need it. Measure out the cornstarch and mix it with a little of the milk to make a slurry. Whip the cream cheese until it is completely smooth, then set aside. Zest and/or juice any citrus fruits. Being prepared makes the whole process easier and more enjoyable. You don't want to be scrambling to find something when the cream base is cooking, for example, or you could overcook and ruin it.

COOK

Almost every ice cream recipe in this book is cooked briefly on the stovetop. Cooking the base provides stability and creaminess in the finished ice cream. While the mixture boils, a set of extraordinary things happens. Sugar liquefies and binds with the water in the milk and cream, which helps to keep the ice cream supple and smooth when frozen. Some water is evaporated out as steam, which concentrates the protein in the mixture and gives the ice cream a thicker, chewier body. Heat also denatures the whey proteins, allowing them to bind with water and prevent ice crystals. Additionally, a small amount of the fat in the cream and milk will also bind with water and prevent iciness in the ice cream. All of this magic happens as the ice cream bubbles away for 4 minutes.

CHILL

The Chill step is what you do after you remove the mixture from the heat. For ice creams, you first slowly stir the hot cream mixture into the awaiting softened cream cheese. Other recipes may call for adding or removing herbs or spices.

The most crucial thing about this step is to ensure that the ice cream mixture cools down quickly. Warm milk and sugar can be a food-safety hazard, because bacteria (some harmful, some not) love to eat sugar and propagate in warm milk. The fastest way to cool the mixture is to pour it into a 1-gallon Ziploc freezer bag, push all the air out, seal it, and submerge it in an ice bath that is heavy on the ice. The bag provides more surface area to cool the mixture more evenly and quickly than any other method, and your base will be ready to freeze in less than 30 minutes. Using a Ball jar instead and giving it a spin in the ice bath every few minutes also works, but you will need a couple of hours for it to chill completely. The traditional bowl set over an ice bath works too, but be careful not to get any water into your ice cream base. You can also chill the mixture overnight in the fridge.

However you do it, it is imperative that the ice cream mixture be below 40°F through and through before you put it in the canister where it will freeze, or it won't work. And if it does not freeze, you will need to remove it from the canister and put it back into the fridge, clean the canister, and freeze it for 12 hours, then try again the next day.

Note: *I don't usually use an ice bath when cooling sorbet mixtures, because these are not very hot and there is less of a food-safety issue than with warm milk and sugar. Instead, you can chill sorbet mixtures right in the fridge, as indicated in the recipes. If you are in a hurry, however, a quick dip in an ice bath will speed up the process.*

FREEZE

If you've just purchased your ice cream machine, you'll need to chill the canister in your freezer for at least 24 hours, so that it becomes fully frozen. Going forward and after washes, it can be chilled for 12 hours, but no less. If possible, store your empty ice cream canisters in the freezer so they remain cold and are always at the ready.

Assemble your ice cream machine, turn it on, and pour in the cold ice cream base, frozen yogurt, or sorbet. Turning the machine on before you pour prevents the mixture from freezing too heavily on the walls of the canister before churning starts. Once the ice cream is churning, you can add any essential oils—since oils can collect on the sides of a plastic bag or bowl, it's better to add them right to the cream when it is in the machine, so they don't get left behind.

Let your ice cream churn for about 20 minutes. I churn it until it is the consistency of soft-serve. Then quickly remove it from the canister and put it into your freezer container. If you want to layer in a variegate or mix-in, do so as you pull the ice cream from the machine. Then cover the surface of the ice cream with parchment paper, get it into the coldest part of your freezer (the back), and freeze for at least 4 hours. (Don't use plastic wrap; it can get caught in any folds and is hard to see and remove.)

Allowing your ice cream to harden fully is an important step. During the time in the freezer, the flavors will open up and bloom into the cream. It takes longer to eat this American-style ice cream than some other ice creams. The warmth of your tongue sweeps a perfect amount off for the flavors to volatilize before going down the hatch, part of the charm of ice cream.

No matter how cold the ice cream gets, the sugar in it never completely freezes. Rather, it becomes attached to the water in the milk and cream and creates an unfrozen semiliquid that keeps the ice cream pliable and elastic when frozen. Otherwise, you would not be able to scoop it.

Scooping   The first trick for scooping ice cream is to choose an oblong container that gives you a runway: flat and long is preferred over deep and round. Depending on how cold your freezer is, you may need to allow your ice cream time to warm up a little before scooping; I let it sit on the counter for about 10 minutes. When you scoop your ice cream, use a dry ice cream scoop, such as a Zeroll scoop. Do not wet it, especially not with hot water. Water will glaze your ice cream with a thin layer of ice. Hot water or a hot scooper will melt the ice cream too much and then the remaining ice cream will crystallize faster when you return it to your freezer. A room-temperature scooper is always the way to go: it will melt just a little bit of ice cream as you run it over the surface, and that will give the scoop enough slide.

Equipment

The equipment needed to make these recipes is all readily available and inexpensive. I created the recipes in this book to use the same size pans—usually a 9-inch round or square pan, a quarter sheet pan, a 4-quart saucepan and other standard kitchen equipment. As for the ice cream machine, it's a must, but there's no need to break the bank.

Ice Cream Machines We used four different models of home ice cream machines to test the recipes in this book: the Cuisinart ICE-21 1½-quart canister machine; the new Breville ice cream bowl attachment, the Freeze & Mix, for its excellent stand mixer (which we have used for years in our test kitchen); Breville's self-contained ice cream maker, the Smart Scoop, and the new Cuisinart soft-serve model ICE-45.

The Cuisinart ICE-21 freezes ice cream 25 percent faster than the ICE-20 model I used for the recipes in my first book. As a result, the ice creams don't get quite enough air whipped in and they come out a little heavier. So with my slight adjustments the recipes in this book will work with either the older or the newer model.

The Breville Freeze & Mix whips quickly and also incorporates quite a bit of air; we regularly got three pints out of each batch with this machine, one more than we got from the Cuisinart. The ice cream is fluffier, but not in a way that detracts from the experience. The stand mixer itself is a great investment—it's the best on the market for a home kitchen.

The Breville self-contained plug-and-play machine makes great ice cream. It can do successive batches with no wait between to freeze the canister, though each succeeding batch will take longer as the housing heats up. The ice creams from this machine are excellent. It comes at a hefty cost ($250 to $400), but if you make ice cream a lot and are happy to have an ice cream machine always at the ready on your counter, it might be a good investment.

Finally, we used the Cuisinart ICE-45. This soft-serve machine is actually exactly the same as the canister machine in terms of spinning and freezing the ice cream, but the ice cream is extruded from underneath the canister through a nozzle. If you practice, you can get really good at dispensing it, which is fun especially for kids, who delight in playing ice cream shop. You can use any of our ice cream recipes in the soft-serve machine, and vice versa.

How does an electric ice cream machine work? The canister is very cold, and the ice cream starts to freeze in thin layers along the inside walls. The dasher spins at a specific rate, scraping the long ice crystals that have built up off the sides of the canister. Those long, jagged ice crystals are forced into the center of the machine, where they tumble around and become smaller, rounded ice crystals, which will be smoother on your tongue. All the while, as the ice cream is churned, a small amount of air is whipped in, which is important for the texture. Without any air, the ice cream will be too compact; too much air, and the ice cream will become powdery.

4-Quart Heavy-Bottomed Saucepan For making ice cream, poaching fruit, and making sauces, a 3½-quart pan will work, but keep a close eye when cooking the milk mixture for ice cream, so it doesn't boil over. Be sure that the pan has a heavy bottom so that it heats evenly.

Baking Sheets and Pans Professional sheet pans and rimmed baking sheets conduct heat evenly and won't burn the bottom of whatever you are baking. They stack together and can be easily stowed away. It's nice to have both half and quarter sheet pans. For the recipes in this book, I also use 9-inch round cake pans and 8-by-8-inch baking dishes.

Whisk A good-quality medium stainless steel whisk is essential for incorporating the milk mixture into the cream cheese, for whipping eggs, and for many other tasks. A balloon whisk is good for whipping cream; it is bigger and has more wires than a regular whisk.

Bowls: Small, Medium, and Large I usually like metal bowls best, but I also have a thing for milk-glass bowls and for the plastic OXO ones with rubber bottoms and pouring spouts. You can use what you like. The important thing is to have at least three mixing bowls, small, medium, and large.

Food Processor A food processor is useful for pulverizing, pureeing, chopping, and the like. It's essential when making Sugar Dough (page 112).

Blender For homogenizing and blending, as in the Crème sans Lait recipe (page 70), a blender works better than a food processor. In this case, any decent brand will suffice.

Freezer Set your freezer on its coldest setting, so that the temperature is 0°F or below. Store ice cream or ice cream desserts in the coldest part of your freezer, the back.

Heatproof Spatulas Heatproof silicone spatulas are unrivaled for stirring ice cream bases and other hot liquids. Buy the one-piece kind, not the type with wooden handles; the wood can rot no matter how often you remove the handle, clean it, and dry it. The wooden-handled ones can also harbor bacteria.

Heavy-Duty 1-Gallon Ziploc Freezer Bags Cooling an ice cream base in a heavy-duty 1-gallon Ziploc freezer bag laid flat in an ice bath is not only the fastest and safest method but also the easiest way to store it. The bag keeps air out and it gives the base a much greater surface area than, say, a jar or a bowl set over an ice bath. Bacteria don't stand a chance, and you're ready to freeze your ice cream in less than 30 minutes.

Ice Cream Scoopers I have two scoopers that I am completely wedded to. The Zeroll scoop has heat-conductive fluid in the handle, which transfers the heat of your hand to the scoop, so the ice cream releases easily. The Rösle scoop is sturdy and sleek, with sharp edges that cut through

ice cream perfectly; it reminds me of those antique metal scoopers that also work well but are usually too covered in rust or limescale to use.

Ice Cream Bar Mold In my opinion, silicone molds are the only way to make ice cream bars. They are easy to fill and it's easier still to remove the bars, so you don't have to melt them to get them out. If you are making J-Bars (page 166), you will need these.

Other Essentials for Every Kitchen
- Bench scraper
- Cheesecloth
- Measuring cups
- Measuring spoons
- Parchment paper
- Pastry bags and tips
- Pie cutter
- Sieve
- Vegetable and "soft-skin" peelers (see Sources, page 200)

Ingredients

Some ingredients vary in composition from brand to brand, which can have an effect on the finished dessert. I used the ingredients below to test all of the recipes in this book. The ice creams and desserts are relatively pure and uncomplicated, so using the finest ingredients you can find, such as grass-fed or organic milk and cream or high-quality chocolate and cocoa, can make all the difference.

Butter My favorite all-purpose butter is Organic Valley cultured butter, because culturing makes some of the lactose (milk sugar) convert to lactic acid, which makes the butter noticeably more flavorful.

Buttermilk For the recipes in this book, buttermilk is always cultured low-fat, which is readily available these days.

Cream Cheese Cream cheese gives these ice creams a little oomph, a little more body. (If you leave it out of these recipes, your ice cream will still be fabulous, just a little thinner.) Use Organic Valley or Philadelphia brands.

Cocoa Powder Dutch-processed cocoa, also known as alkalized, is very round, full, soft, and complex. "Dutch process" means the cocoa has been treated in order to make it more water-soluble—so it will quickly dissolve into your sugar syrup. Cocoa that has not been Dutch-processed, sometimes called natural cocoa, is sharper, more earthy, and a softer brown. Despite being lighter in color, it can have a darker flavor. Many people don't like it as much as Dutch-processed chocolate, but I love it in certain ice creams. You can choose whichever you prefer for these recipes.

Light Corn Syrup In ice creams and in baking, we use corn syrup as a humectant, for its water-attracting quality, which comes from glucose, not fructose. Adding a bit of corn syrup in place of table sugar actually makes the ice cream less sweet. Look for regular light corn syrup, without high fructose. Fructose makes the syrup sweeter— you don't want that.

Self-Rising Flour Self-rising flour is just flour with baking powder and salt added. You can make your own by adding 1½ teaspoons baking powder and ¼ teaspoon salt to every cup of flour in the recipe and sifting them together.

Gluten-Free Flour We use two different brands of gluten-free flour, Pamela's and Cup 4 Cup, to test these recipes. Pamela's Baking Mix also works in a pinch and may be easier to find.

Sugar We use only white cane sugar, not beet sugar. Beet sugar burns too easily. The ice creams we sell in our shops and online are made with vegan sugar. Muscovado, light or dark brown, or palm sugar can all be used instead, but remember your ice cream will take on the flavor of the sugar you choose.

Ice Cream Parlor

Ice cream is not simply a dessert, it's a moment. You can spend all day picking out a flavor, but once you do, you have no choice but to be present with it. Engage with it. Lick it before it melts down your arm.

———

It's not just beautiful flavors that make ice cream such a delight. If you start with good ingredients, it will surely taste good. But the real work of an ice cream maker begins with texture and body. Because if the ice cream is icy, soupy, crumbly, or thin, the whole experience becomes forgettable. I spend a lot of time thinking of new flavors, but I spend more worrying about texture. If an idea for a new flavor is what gets me up in the morning, it's the textural issues that keep me up at night. It's not great ice cream unless flavor, texture, body, and finish are all in sync. That's hard to achieve when using fresh ingredients, because everything you add to ice cream upsets the balance.

In this chapter, I give you my improved classic ice cream and frozen yogurt bases, a brand-new rich and silky custard base, and a killer vegan base called Crème sans Lait. I cannot say enough about Crème sans Lait. It's super-creamy and scoopable, with surprising dairy flavor. You can make it in so many flavors that anyone is sure to love it, even if it is vegan. With these four bases as your tools, you can make smooth, dense, dreamy, delicious scoops to adorn your desserts. Use them to make the ice creams straight out of this chapter, or mix and match from the other chapters in this book (or in *Jeni's Splendid Ice Creams at Home*) and layer flavors and textures to create your own unique ice creams.

When crafting your own flavors, it's usually good to keep it simple. I rarely do more than two or three flavors layered in one ice cream. Occasionally, I'll add something crunchy and a sauce. Flavors that have too much going on feel cluttered. The goal is to strike a perfect balance and if you do, the flavor will taste and feel like a symphony, with everything unfolding at the right moment.

All of the ice creams in this chapter can be used in many ways. My recipe for Salty Vanilla Frozen Custard (page 60) is tailor-made for filling Éclairs or Cream Puffs (page 130). But it also can be a rich, eggy frozen custard base for other flavors—just add a handful of chopped nuts, a sprinkling of Gravel (pages 194–97), or some cake crumbles. One of my favorite new flavors of the past couple of years is Absinthe & Meringue (page 30), which we made to celebrate the hundredth anniversary of Igor Stravinsky's groundbreaking work *The Rite of Spring*. When you add a couple of drops of bitters and some crushed orange candies in the mix, you get Triumph Ice Cream (page 31), which is inspired by the vintage cocktail of the same name. This lovely variation makes the perfect digestif and dessert in one.

The point is, the flavors are now yours. Make them straight up, or pull elements from other flavors, other chapters in this book, or from the recipes in my first book, to create your very own flavors. You have the keys to the kingdom!

SWEET CREAM ICE CREAM

My classic ice cream base. I also love it on its own.

This is your new and improved go-to ice cream base. I updated and tweaked it from the base recipe in my first book to accommodate new ice cream machines, but it also works just as well in the older or even vintage models.

You will find that it is smooth and creamy with a beautifully scoopable body. This Sweet Cream Ice Cream is the base for many of the ice cream recipes in this book—it can be used to make any flavor you wish. It is wonderful by itself or in a sundae or with any sauce or jam layered throughout.

You can customize this and other ice creams with the addition of essential oils and extracts, fruits, herbs, spices, nuts, crumbled cakes, cookies, and gravel, as well as jams and sauces (see To Add Variegates, opposite). When using essential oils, go lightly and taste often—usually just 2 to 5 drops will do.

The simplest flavors are often the finest. One of our all-time biggest hits, and one of my personal favorites, is the variation presented here, where the Sweet Cream Ice Cream is swirled with Blackberry Jam.

Makes about 1 quart

2⅔ cups whole milk

1 tablespoon plus 2 teaspoons cornstarch

2 ounces (4 tablespoons) cream cheese, softened

⅛ teaspoon fine sea salt

1½ cups heavy cream

¾ cup sugar

¼ cup light corn syrup

Sweet Cream Ice Cream with Blackberry Jam
As you pack the ice cream into a storage container, layer in ½ cup of chilled Blackberry Jam (page 182).

PREP Mix about 2 tablespoons of the milk with the cornstarch in a small bowl to make a smooth slurry.

Whisk the cream cheese and salt in a medium bowl until smooth. Fill a large bowl with ice and water.

COOK Combine the remaining milk, the cream, sugar, and corn syrup in a 4-quart saucepan, bring to a boil over medium-high heat, and boil for 4 minutes. Remove from the heat and gradually whisk in the cornstarch slurry. Bring the mixture back to a boil over medium-high heat and cook, stirring with a heatproof spatula, until slightly thickened, about 1 minute. Remove from the heat.

CHILL Gradually whisk the hot milk mixture into the cream cheese until smooth. Pour the mixture into a 1-gallon Ziploc freezer bag and submerge the sealed bag in the ice bath. Let stand, adding more ice as necessary, until cold, about 30 minutes.

FREEZE Remove the frozen canister from the freezer, assemble your ice cream machine, and turn it on. Pour the ice cream base into the canister and spin until thick and creamy.

Pack the ice cream into a storage container. Press a sheet of parchment directly against the surface and seal with an airtight lid. Freeze in the coldest part of your freezer until firm, at least 4 hours.

To Add Variegates: For layering jams or sauces into ice cream, start by drizzling a spoonful into the bottom of the storage container and spreading a layer of ice cream over it. Add a few more spoonfuls into the nooks of the ice cream, and then add another ice cream layer. Continue the sauce and ice cream layering until all the ice cream is used. The sauce should not cover the whole layer. Note that you do not want to "swirl" in the sauce because it will get lost in the ice cream altogether; instead, try to keep it in small pockets throughout the ice cream for a more dramatic presentation and flavor. I also like to add a few final spoonfuls on the top for decoration, just before covering with parchment.

ABSINTHE & MERINGUE ICE CREAM

Absinthe imparts a mild licorice flavor; airy, sweet meringue adds lightness; and matcha powder imbues color and a crisp finish.

The year 2013 marked the one hundredth anniversary of Igor Stravinsky's symphony, with accompanying ballet, *The Rite of Spring*. We created Absinthe & Meringue Ice Cream for the Columbus Symphony Orchestra and BalletMet's production that spring to help take the audience back to the time of its debut in Paris in 1913.

The Rite of Spring is a story about primitive desires, emotions, and reactions. It was in stark contrast to the way of life of most upper-class Parisians. The highly charged production knocked them straight off their rockers. Bohemians, however, applauded the production's boldness and break with tradition. The tension between the upper and bohemian classes caused a near-riot at the ballet's premiere, but the symphony would change music and tastes forever.

Absinthe & Meringue Ice Cream is a clash of flavors and textures. The absinthe, with its notorious reputation, represents the uncontrollable emotions of spring. The meticulously piped, pretty, fussy meringue kisses represent the effort, especially by the upper classes during the early 1900s, to control everything in nature. That they get crushed by the weight of the absinthe cream is the conclusion of the story that we are still enjoying today in the form of jazz, rock 'n' roll, punk, and modernism in general, which are all, to some extent, the legacy of *The Rite of Spring*.

Makes about 1 quart

2⅔ cups whole milk

1 tablespoon plus 2 teaspoons cornstarch

2 ounces (4 tablespoons) cream cheese, softened

½ teaspoon matcha powder (see Sources, page 200)

⅛ teaspoon fine sea salt

1½ cups heavy cream

¾ cup sugar

¼ cup light corn syrup

¼ cup absinthe, Pernod, or pastis (see Sources, page 200)

½ teaspoon anise extract

1 cup crumbled (about ¼-inch crumbles) meringue from Meringue Cake (page 102; about 1 Meringue) or store-bought

PREP Mix about 2 tablespoons of the milk with the cornstarch in a small bowl to make a smooth slurry.

Whisk the cream cheese, matcha, and salt in a medium bowl until smooth.

Fill a large bowl with ice and water.

COOK Combine the remaining milk, the cream, sugar, and corn syrup in a 4-quart saucepan, bring to a boil over medium-high heat, and boil for 4 minutes. Remove from the heat and gradually whisk in the cornstarch slurry. Bring the mixture back to a boil over medium-high heat and cook, stirring with a heatproof spatula, until slightly thickened, about 1 minute. Remove from the heat.

CHILL Gradually whisk the hot milk mixture into the cream cheese until smooth. Pour the mixture into a 1-gallon Ziploc freezer bag and submerge the sealed bag in the ice bath. Let stand, adding more ice as necessary, until cold, about 30 minutes.

FREEZE Remove the frozen canister from the freezer, assemble your ice cream machine, and turn it on. Pour the ice cream base into the canister and spin until thick and creamy.

Pack the ice cream into a storage container. Stir in the absinthe and anise extract and mix in the meringue pieces as you go. Press a sheet of parchment directly against the surface and seal with an airtight lid. Freeze in the coldest part of your freezer until firm, at least 4 hours.

Triumph Ice Cream

One of my favorite cocktails is the Triumph: absinthe with egg whites and blood orange. Make it into ice cream! Add a generous dash of orange bitters to the Absinthe & Meringue base, then add crushed blood orange hard candies as you pack the ice cream into the storage container.

BLACK FOREST CAKE ICE CREAM

Tangy buttermilk ice cream loaded with crumbles of dense chocolate cake, chocolate sauce, and Amarena cherries.

One of our most popular flavors ever, this ice cream has a base made with buttermilk and cream that is reminiscent of crème fraîche, with crumbles of chocolate cake soaked in chocolate sauce, and Amarena cherries strewn throughout. Amarena cherries are wild cherries that grow in the Calabria region of Italy. The ones we buy are candied or preserved in syrup by a company called Fabbri and we use them for many things. Plain frozen yogurt made with Amarena cherries is exquisite. They are a great option when a recipe calls for maraschino cherries and you're craving something special.

Makes about 1 quart

⅔ cup crumbled (½-inch crumbles) A Wiseman's Chocolate Cake (page 98), frozen, or from a store-bought chocolate cake

¼ cup Runny Chocolate Sauce (page 190), chilled

½ cup Amarena cherries (see Sources, page 200)

1¼ cups heavy cream

2 tablespoons cornstarch

3 ounces (6 tablespoons) cream cheese, softened

¼ teaspoon fine sea salt

⅔ cup sugar

2 tablespoons light corn syrup

2 cups buttermilk, whole milk, or 2% milk

ADVANCE PREP Put the cake crumbles in a small bowl, add the chocolate sauce, and toss lightly to coat, then add the Amarena cherries and stir to distribute evenly. Freeze while you make the ice cream. (The cake mixture can be frozen for up to 1 month.)

PREP Mix about ¼ cup of the cream with the cornstarch in a small bowl to make a smooth slurry.

Whisk the cream cheese and salt in a medium bowl until smooth. Fill a large bowl with ice and water.

COOK Combine the remaining cream, the sugar, and corn syrup in a 4-quart saucepan, bring to a boil over medium-high heat, and boil for 4 minutes. Remove from the heat and gradually whisk in the cornstarch slurry. Bring the mixture back to a boil over medium-high heat and cook, stirring with a heatproof spatula, until slightly thickened, about 20 seconds. Remove from the heat.

CHILL Gradually whisk the hot milk mixture into the cream cheese until smooth, then stir in the buttermilk. Pour the mixture into a 1-gallon Ziploc bag and submerge the sealed bag in the ice bath. Let stand, adding more ice as necessary, until cold, about 30 minutes.

FREEZE Remove the frozen canister from the freezer, assemble your ice cream machine, and turn it on. Pour the ice cream base into the canister and spin until thick and creamy.

Pack the ice cream into a storage container, alternating the ice cream and small spoonfuls of the cake mixture. Press a sheet of parchment directly against the surface and seal with an airtight lid. Freeze in the coldest part of your freezer until firm, at least 4 hours.

FARMSTEAD CHEESE & GUAVA JAM ICE CREAM

Fresh, soft farmstead cheese makes a wonderful cheesecake ice cream.

Cloverton is a soft farmstead cheese from Laurel Valley Creamery, a family-owned farm on the Ohio River in southern Ohio. We love the cheese for its ultrarich creaminess, and we use it often in our ice creams. If you can't find a similar soft cheese at your local cheese shop, use extra cream cheese in this recipe.

One of my favorite ways to make this ice cream is to swirl in some Guava Jam, inspired by a dessert of soft Cuban cheese and slices of ripe guava that I had in Little Havana when I lived in Miami twenty years ago.

Make it into a cheesecake by sprinkling in ½ cup Salty Graham Gravel (page 195) and adding a swirl of Red Currant–Strawberry Sauce (page 185) or White House Cherries (page 186).

Makes about 1 quart

2⅔ cups whole milk

1 tablespoon plus 2 teaspoons cornstarch

6 ounces (¾ cup) Cloverton cheese (or any soft farmstead cheese; see Sources, page 200) or cream cheese, softened

⅛ teaspoon fine sea salt

1½ cups heavy cream

¾ cup sugar

¼ cup light corn syrup

½ cup Guava Jam (page 182)

Beet Lady Cake Ice Cream
Think of this ice cream as a carrot cake only with beets. The cheese ice cream is like the frosting. Substitute ⅔ cup crumbled Beet Lady Cake (page 100) for the Guava Jam.

PREP Mix about 2 tablespoons of the milk with the cornstarch in a small bowl to make a smooth slurry.

Whisk the cheese and salt in a medium bowl until smooth.

Fill a large bowl with ice and water.

COOK Combine the remaining milk, the cream, sugar, and corn syrup in a 4-quart saucepan, bring to a boil over medium-high heat, and boil for 4 minutes. Remove from the heat and gradually whisk in the cornstarch slurry. Bring the mixture back to a boil over medium-high heat and cook, stirring with a heatproof spatula, until slightly thickened, about 1 minute. Remove from the heat.

CHILL Gradually whisk the hot milk mixture into the cheese until smooth. Pour the mixture into a 1-gallon Ziploc freezer bag and submerge the sealed bag in the ice bath. Let stand, adding more ice as necessary, until cold, about 30 minutes.

FREEZE Remove the frozen canister from the freezer, assemble your ice cream machine, and turn it on. Pour the ice cream base into the frozen canister and spin until thick and creamy.

Pack the ice cream into a storage container, layering in the jam as you go. Press a sheet of parchment directly against the surface and seal with an airtight lid. Freeze in the coldest part of your freezer until firm, at least 4 hours.

CREAM BISCUITS WITH PEACH JAM ICE CREAM

Buttermilk ice cream loaded with tender crumbled biscuits and fragrant Peach Jam.

We have two scoop shops in Nashville, so I'm there a lot; I consider it my second home. On the days I go to Nashville, I grab my carry-on rucksack, skip breakfast or coffee, and head to the Columbus airport. When I arrive at 7:00 in Nashville, I am still waking up as I make my way to the rental car. As soon as I get into town, I head to one of my many favorite breakfast or coffee joints, like the Barista Parlor or Fido. On days when I feel like driving a little bit farther, I'll head to the Loveless Cafe.

This ice cream was inspired by the cafe's famous biscuits, which they serve with every meal. Everyone falls for them. You get three little biscuits served with the Loveless's homemade jams. I think that everything in the restaurant comes with a side of these off-the-charts-good biscuits. They never share their recipe—not even in their own cookbook! But, our Sweet Cream Shortcakes work great in this recipe, swirled with our homemade Peach Jam into a fitting buttermilk base. This flavor has Loveless Cafe's blessing—and that's good enough for us.

Makes about 1 quart

- 1¼ cups heavy cream
- 2 tablespoons cornstarch
- 3 ounces (6 tablespoons) cream cheese, softened
- ¼ teaspoon fine sea salt
- ⅔ cup sugar
- 2 tablespoons light corn syrup
- 2 cups buttermilk, whole milk, or 2% milk
- ½ cup crumbled Sweet Cream Shortcakes (page 124), frozen, or store-bought biscuits
- ¼ cup Peach Jam (page 183), chilled

PREP Mix about ¼ cup of the cream with the cornstarch in a small bowl to make a smooth slurry.

Whisk the cream cheese and salt in a medium bowl until smooth.

Fill a large bowl with ice and water.

COOK Combine the remaining cream, the sugar, and corn syrup in a 4-quart saucepan, bring to a boil over medium-high heat, and boil for 4 minutes. Remove from the heat and gradually whisk in the cornstarch slurry. Bring the mixture back to a boil over medium-high heat and cook, stirring with a heatproof spatula, until slightly thickened, about 20 seconds. Remove from the heat.

CHILL Gradually whisk the hot milk mixture into the cream cheese until smooth. Stir in the buttermilk.

Pour the mixture into a 1-gallon Ziploc bag and submerge the sealed bag in the ice bath. Let stand, adding more ice as necessary, until cold, about 30 minutes.

FREEZE Remove the frozen canister from the freezer, assemble your ice cream machine, and turn it on. Pour the ice cream base into the frozen canister and spin until thick and creamy.

Pack the ice cream into a storage container, mixing in the crumbled biscuits and jam as you go. Press a sheet of parchment directly against the surface and seal with an airtight lid. Freeze in the coldest part of your freezer until firm, at least 4 hours.

CUMIN & HONEY BUTTERSCOTCH ICE CREAM

Toasted cumin and caramelized honey: smoky, aromatic, and highly addictive.

Honey and cumin are some of the oldest ingredients known to have been used to flavor food. Cumin is smoky and takes to the earthy sweetness of honey effortlessly. We caramelize the honey slightly, which further melds the two flavors. This ice cream is both ancient and magical.

PREP Mix about 2 tablespoons of the milk with the cornstarch in a small bowl to make a smooth slurry.

Whisk the cream cheese, salt, turmeric, if using, and cumin in a medium bowl until smooth.

Fill a large bowl with ice and water.

COOK Heat the honey in a 4-quart saucepan over medium-high heat until it begins to boil and just begins to smoke. Remove the pan from the heat and stir in about ¼ cup of the cream. Slowly add the rest of the cream, stirring until incorporated.

Add the remaining milk and the sugar to the pan, bring to a boil over medium-high heat, and boil for 4 minutes. Remove from the heat and gradually whisk in the cornstarch slurry. Bring the mixture back to a boil over medium-high heat and cook, stirring with a heatproof spatula, until slightly thickened, about 1 minute. Remove from the heat.

CHILL Gradually whisk the hot milk mixture into the cream cheese until smooth. Pour the mixture into a 1-gallon Ziploc freezer bag and submerge the sealed bag in the ice bath. Let stand, adding more ice as necessary, until cold, about 30 minutes. Stir in the butter flavoring.

FREEZE Remove the frozen canister from the freezer, assemble your ice cream machine, and turn it on. Pour the ice cream base into the canister and spin until thick and creamy.

Pack the ice cream into a storage container. Press a sheet of parchment directly against the surface and seal with an airtight lid. Freeze in the coldest part of your freezer until firm, at least 4 hours.

Makes about 1 quart

- 2⅔ cups whole milk
- 1 tablespoon plus 2 teaspoons cornstarch
- 2 ounces (4 tablespoons) cream cheese, softened
- ¼ teaspoon fine sea salt
- 1 teaspoon turmeric (for color; optional)
- ¼ teaspoon ground cumin
- ½ cup honey
- 1½ cups heavy cream
- ½ cup sugar
- 4 drops natural butter flavoring (see Sources, page 200)

JUNIPER & LEMON CURD ICE CREAM

As coolly invigorating and bracing as the first sip of a day-capping martini.

Here you get lush cream with the zing of crystal-clear juniper and swirls of sweet-tart lemon curd.

We go easy on the juniper essential oil, because it is strong and will bloom even more as the ice cream ages, and go heavy on the Lemon Curd, because it's delicious.

PREP Mix about 2 tablespoons of the milk with the cornstarch in a small bowl to make a smooth slurry.

Whisk the cream cheese and salt in a medium bowl until smooth. Fill a large bowl with ice and water.

COOK Combine the remaining milk, the cream, sugar, and corn syrup in a 4-quart saucepan, bring to a boil over medium-high heat, and boil for 4 minutes. Remove from the heat and gradually whisk in the cornstarch slurry. Bring the mixture back to a boil over medium-high heat and cook, stirring with a heatproof spatula, until slightly thickened, about 1 minute. Remove from the heat.

CHILL Gradually whisk the hot milk mixture into the cream cheese until smooth. Pour the mixture into a 1-gallon Ziploc freezer bag and submerge the sealed bag in the ice bath. Let stand, adding more ice as necessary, until cold, about 30 minutes.

FREEZE Remove the frozen canister from the freezer, assemble your ice cream machine, and turn it on. Pour the ice cream base into the canister and add the juniper oil. Spin until thick and creamy.

Pack the ice cream into a storage container, layering in the lemon curd as you go. Press a sheet of parchment directly against the surface, and seal with an airtight lid. Freeze in the coldest part of your freezer until firm, at least 4 hours.

Makes about 1 quart

2⅔ cups whole milk

1 tablespoon plus 2 teaspoons cornstarch

2 ounces (4 tablespoons) cream cheese, softened

⅛ teaspoon fine sea salt

1½ cups heavy cream

¾ cup sugar

¼ cup light corn syrup

1 to 2 drops juniper essential oil

⅔ cup Lemon Curd (page 183)

DARK CHOCOLATE &
RYE WHISKEY ICE CREAM

A drunken dark chocolate, with notes of caraway.

If I had to pick my three favorite ingredients of all time, I'd go with whiskey, caraway, and chocolate. Rye whiskey is a very nice addition to chocolate, and although rye does not have flavors of caraway, the combination seems natural—mostly because we associate the two with rye bread. We made this ice cream to honor Zelda Fitzgerald's experience in the early 1920s in St. Paul, Minnesota, with her husband, Scott.

Rye was popular before Prohibition but then went out of fashion and became relatively rare. Today it's making a big comeback at small distilleries, and I'm happy to be aboard that train.

Makes about 1 quart

CHOCOLATE PASTE

½ cup brewed coffee
  (any temperature)

¼ cup sugar

⅔ cup Dutch-processed cocoa
  powder

1½ ounces unsweetened chocolate,
  finely chopped

ICE CREAM BASE

2⅔ cups whole milk

1 tablespoon plus 2 teaspoons
  cornstarch

2 ounces (4 tablespoons)
  cream cheese, softened

⅛ teaspoon fine sea salt

1½ cups heavy cream

¾ cup sugar

3 tablespoons light corn syrup

3 tablespoons caraway seeds,
  lightly crushed

½ cup rye whiskey

ADVANCE PREP

For the chocolate paste
Combine the coffee, sugar, and cocoa in a small saucepan, bring to a boil over medium heat, and boil for 30 seconds, stirring to dissolve the sugar. Remove from the heat and add the chocolate. Let stand for a few minutes, then stir until very smooth.

PREP Mix about 2 tablespoons of the milk with the cornstarch in a small bowl to make a smooth slurry.

Whisk the cream cheese, warm chocolate paste, and salt in a medium bowl until smooth.

Fill a large bowl with ice and water.

COOK Combine the remaining milk, the cream, sugar, and corn syrup in a 4-quart saucepan and bring to a boil over medium-high heat. Stir in the caraway seeds and boil for 4 minutes. Remove from the heat and gradually whisk in the cornstarch slurry. Bring the mixture back to a boil over medium-high heat and cook, stirring with a heatproof spatula, until slightly thickened, about 1 minute. Remove from the heat.

CHILL Gradually whisk the hot milk mixture into the cream cheese mixture until smooth. Stir in the whiskey. Pour the mixture into a 1-gallon Ziploc freezer bag and submerge the sealed bag in the ice bath. Let stand, adding more ice as necessary, until cold, about 30 minutes.

FREEZE Remove the frozen canister from the freezer, assemble your ice cream machine, and turn it on. Pour the ice cream base into the frozen canister and spin until thick and creamy.

Pack the ice cream into a storage container. Press a sheet of parchment directly against the surface, and seal with an airtight lid. Freeze in the coldest part of your freezer until firm, at least 4 hours.

DOUBLE-TOASTED COCONUT–CAJETA ICE CREAM

Cream with flecks of golden brown coconut and cajeta layered throughout.

I think of this flavor as a guilty pleasure, like a candy bar. In fact, it would be outstanding in a J-Bar (page 166): molded onto a stick, with a river of cajeta (goat's-milk caramel) down the middle of the ice cream, then coated in chocolate.

When you toast the coconut, be sure to get it evenly browned. Raw unsweetened coconut has little to no flavor when frozen. You need every single fleck to be golden brown in order to infuse your ice cream with flavor. When I say double-toasted coconut, I mean extra-toasted: it should be very caramelized.

Makes about 1 quart

½ cup unsweetened coconut flakes

2⅔ cups whole milk

1 tablespoon plus 2 teaspoons cornstarch

2 ounces (4 tablespoons) cream cheese, softened

⅛ teaspoon fine sea salt

1½ cups heavy cream

¾ cup sugar

¼ cup light corn syrup

2 to 3 drops coconut extract (optional)

⅓ cup Cajeta (page 187)

ADVANCE PREP

For the coconut

Preheat the oven to 325°F.

Spread the coconut on a baking sheet. Toast for 10 minutes, then remove from the oven and toss with a heatproof spatula, making sure to bring the outside edges of the coconut in toward the inner less-toasted portion. Spread out and toast for 5 more minutes, then toss again. Repeat until the coconut is evenly golden brown and very fragrant. Remove from the oven and let cool completely.

PREP Mix about 2 tablespoons of the milk with the cornstarch in a small bowl to make a smooth slurry.

Whisk the cream cheese and salt in a medium bowl until smooth.

Fill a large bowl with ice and water.

COOK Combine the remaining milk, the cream, sugar, and corn syrup in a 4-quart saucepan, bring to a boil over medium-high heat, and boil for 4 minutes. Remove from the heat and gradually whisk in the cornstarch slurry. Bring the mixture back to a boil over medium-high heat and cook, stirring with a heatproof spatula, until slightly thickened, about 1 minute. Remove from the heat.

CHILL Gradually whisk the hot milk mixture into the cream cheese until smooth. Add the coconut extract, if using. Pour the mixture into a 1-gallon Ziploc freezer bag and submerge the sealed bag in the ice bath. Let stand, adding more ice as necessary, until cold, about 30 minutes.

FREEZE Remove the frozen canister from the freezer, assemble your ice cream machine, and turn it on. Pour the ice cream base into the canister and spin until thick and creamy.

Pack the ice cream into a storage container, mixing in the toasted coconut and layering in the sauce as you go. Press a sheet of parchment directly against the surface and seal with an airtight lid. Freeze in the coldest part of your freezer until firm, at least 4 hours.

EXTRA-STRENGTH
ROOT BEER ICE CREAM

Like the sweet, creamy, frothy foam atop a frosty mug of ice-cold root beer.

The root beer concentrate that we use is from Frostop, our local root beer maker, and it's super-creamy, with just the right amount of birch and vanilla. We also like Sprecher's. Just pick a concentrate or root beer flavoring that smells good to you, and then use it to make the ice cream as intensely flavorful as you like (taste as you go).

Turn the traditional root beer float on its head: Extra-Strength Root Beer Ice Cream and cream soda topped with whipped cream in a frozen glass.

PREP Mix about 2 tablespoons of the milk with the cornstarch in a small bowl to make a smooth slurry.

Whisk the cream cheese and salt in a medium bowl until smooth.

Fill a large bowl with ice and water.

COOK Combine the remaining milk, the cream, sugar, and corn syrup in a 4-quart saucepan, bring to a boil over medium-high heat, and boil for 4 minutes. Remove from the heat and gradually whisk in the cornstarch slurry. Bring the mixture back to a boil over medium-high heat and cook, stirring with a heatproof spatula, until slightly thickened, about 1 minute. Remove from the heat.

CHILL Gradually whisk the hot milk mixture into the cream cheese until smooth. Add the root beer concentrate. Pour the mixture into a 1-gallon Ziploc freezer bag and submerge the sealed bag in the ice bath. Let stand, adding more ice as necessary, until cold, about 30 minutes.

FREEZE Remove the frozen canister from the freezer, assemble your ice cream machine, and turn it on. Pour the ice cream base into the frozen canister and spin until thick and creamy.

Pack the ice cream into a storage container. Press a sheet of parchment directly against the surface and seal with an airtight lid. Freeze in the coldest part of your freezer until firm, at least 4 hours.

Makes about 1 quart

2⅔ cups whole milk

1 tablespoon plus 2 teaspoons cornstarch

2 ounces (4 tablespoons) cream cheese, softened

⅛ teaspoon fine sea salt

1½ cups heavy cream

¾ cup sugar

¼ cup light corn syrup

2 tablespoons root beer concentrate or extract, or to taste, depending on its strength (see Sources, page 200)

MAGNOLIA MOCHI ICE CREAM

Sweet and subtly floral magnolia-scented ice cream melts on the tongue, revealing cubes of springy Mochi Cake.

We created this flavor for our Super Pop Cakes collection. The idea behind the collection was that cakes are to dessert as pop is to music: easy to love, bright in color, and shimmering in tone. Magnolia ice cream, made with magnolia essential oil and colored a vibrant pastel pink with beet powder and turmeric, is also glorious without the mochi.

PREP Mix about 2 tablespoons of the milk with the cornstarch in a small bowl to make a smooth slurry.

Whisk the cream cheese, beet powder and turmeric if using, and salt in a medium bowl until smooth.

Fill a large bowl with ice and water.

COOK Combine the remaining milk, the cream, sugar, and corn syrup in a 4-quart saucepan, bring to a boil over medium-high heat, and boil for 4 minutes. Remove from the heat and gradually whisk in the cornstarch slurry. Bring the mixture back to a boil over medium-high heat and cook, stirring with a heatproof spatula, until slightly thickened, about 1 minute. Remove from the heat.

CHILL Gradually whisk the hot milk mixture into the cream cheese until smooth. Pour the mixture into a 1-gallon Ziploc freezer bag and submerge the sealed bag in the ice bath. Let stand, adding more ice as necessary, until cold, about 30 minutes.

FREEZE Remove the frozen canister from the freezer, assemble your ice cream machine, and turn it on. Pour the ice cream base into the canister, add the magnolia essential oil, and spin until thick and creamy.

Pack the ice cream into a storage container, mixing in the cake cubes as you go. Press a sheet of parchment directly against the surface and seal with an airtight lid. Freeze in the coldest part of your freezer until firm, at least 4 hours.

Makes about 1 quart

- 2⅔ cups whole milk
- 1 tablespoon plus 2 teaspoons cornstarch
- 2 ounces (4 tablespoons) cream cheese, softened
- 1 tablespoon red beet powder (for color; see Sources, page 200; optional)
- ¼ teaspoon turmeric (for color; optional)
- ⅛ teaspoon fine sea salt
- 1½ cups heavy cream
- ¾ cup sugar
- ¼ cup light corn syrup
- 1 to 2 drops magnolia essential oil
- ½ cup ⅛-inch cubes Mochi Cake (page 104), frozen

GRAHAM CRACKER ICE CREAM

Salty, sweet, buttery graham cracker ice cream.

If I asked you to describe the flavor of graham crackers, what would you say? It takes some thinking: kind of malty, buttery, sweet, caramelized. When you eat a graham cracker, you might be taken back to your childhood, or to a time when you ate a fantastic key lime pie. Well, this ice cream is all of that. It's both familiar and incredibly awesome. Though its uses in composed desserts are many, we also love it by itself in a cone. In a bowl with some bananas, it's a dream.

Substituting animal crackers for the grahams makes for an ice cream that is again both familiar and indescribably delicious.

Makes about 1 quart

2⅔ cups whole milk

1 tablespoon plus 2 teaspoons cornstarch

2 ounces (4 tablespoons) cream cheese, softened

⅛ teaspoon fine sea salt

1½ cups heavy cream

¾ cup sugar

¼ cup light corn syrup

½ cup roughly chopped (¼-inch pieces) graham crackers, preferably Annie's Honey Bunny (see Sources, page 200)

Blue Cheese Graham Cracker Ice Cream
Substitute Gorgonzola dolce for the cream cheese. The result will be a little saltier, and the cheese will bring out the caramel notes.

PREP Mix about 2 tablespoons of the milk with the cornstarch in a small bowl to make a smooth slurry.

Whisk the cream cheese and salt in a medium bowl until smooth. Fill a large bowl with ice and water.

COOK Combine the remaining milk, the cream, sugar, and corn syrup in a 4-quart saucepan, bring to a boil over medium-high heat, and boil for 4 minutes. Remove from the heat and gradually whisk in the cornstarch slurry. Bring the mixture back to a boil over medium-high heat and cook, stirring with a heatproof spatula, until slightly thickened, about 1 minute. Remove from the heat.

CHILL Gradually whisk the hot milk mixture into the cream cheese until smooth. Add the crackers and allow the mixture to steep until the crackers dissolve, about 3 minutes. Force the mixture through a sieve, then pour it into a 1-gallon Ziploc freezer bag and submerge the sealed bag in the ice bath. Let stand, adding more ice as necessary, until cold, about 30 minutes.

FREEZE Remove the frozen canister from the freezer, assemble your ice cream machine, and turn it on. Pour the ice cream base into the frozen canister and spin until thick and creamy.

Pack the ice cream into a storage container. Press a sheet of parchment directly against the surface and seal with an airtight lid. Freeze in the coldest part of your freezer until firm, at least 4 hours.

Animal Cracker Ice Cream
For an ice cream that is both familiar and indescribably delicious, substitute animal crackers for the graham crackers.

HONEYED BUTTERMILK ICE CREAM WITH CORN BREAD GRAVEL

Sweet and tangy and crunchy.

The buttermilk gives this ice cream a bright cultured dairy flavor, while the caramelization brings out the flavor of the honey. Honey Corn Bread Gravel is the perfect complement, with a pinch of cayenne pepper.

PREP Mix about 2 tablespoons of the buttermilk with the cornstarch in a small bowl to make a smooth slurry.

Whisk the cream cheese, salt, and turmeric, if using, and cayenne pepper in a medium bowl until smooth.

Fill a large bowl with ice and water.

COOK Heat the honey in a 4-quart saucepan over medium-high heat until it begins to boil and just begins to smoke. Remove the pan from the heat and stir in about ¼ cup of the cream. Slowly add the rest of the cream, stirring until incorporated.

Add the remaining buttermilk, bring to a boil over medium-high heat, and boil for 4 minutes. Remove from the heat and gradually whisk in the cornstarch slurry. Bring the mixture back to a boil over medium-high heat and cook, stirring with a heatproof spatula, until slightly thickened, about 1 minute. Remove from the heat.

CHILL Gradually whisk the hot milk mixture into the cream cheese until smooth. Pour the mixture into a 1-gallon Ziploc freezer bag and submerge the sealed bag in the ice bath. Let stand, adding more ice as necessary, until cold, about 30 minutes.

FREEZE Remove the frozen canister from the freezer, assemble your ice cream machine, and turn it on. Pour the ice cream base into the frozen canister and spin until thick and creamy.

Pack the ice cream into a storage container, mixing in the corn bread gravel as you go. Press a sheet of parchment directly against the surface and seal with an airtight lid. Freeze in the coldest part of your freezer until firm, at least 4 hours.

Makes about 1 quart

2 cups buttermilk

1 tablespoon plus 2 teaspoons cornstarch

2 ounces (4 tablespoons) cream cheese, softened

¼ teaspoon fine sea salt

½ teaspoon turmeric (for color; optional)

Pinch of cayenne pepper, or to taste

⅔ cup honey

1½ cups heavy cream

½ cup Honey Corn Bread Gravel (page 197)

PUMPERNICKEL ICE CREAM

Caraway-infused sweet ice cream with salty Pumpernickel Gravel throughout.

Pumpernickel is one of my favorite ice creams, and it's also one of my favorite flavors. We spent time in Germany when I was a little girl, and I am sure that my taste for it is rooted in those memories. You can toss in some Pumpernickel Gravel to give this ice cream even more character. It's also fantastic with some tart red cherries or bitter orange marmalade swirled in.

PREP Mix about 2 tablespoons of the milk with the cornstarch in a small bowl to make a smooth slurry.
Whisk the cream cheese and salt in a medium bowl until smooth. Fill a large bowl with ice and water.

COOK Combine the remaining milk, the cream, sugar, molasses, and corn syrup in a 4-quart saucepan, bring to a boil over medium-high heat, and boil for 4 minutes. Remove from the heat and gradually whisk in the cornstarch slurry. Bring the mixture back to a boil over medium-high heat and cook, stirring with a heatproof spatula, until slightly thickened, about 1 minute. Remove from the heat.

CHILL Gradually whisk the hot milk mixture into the cream cheese until smooth. Pour the mixture into a 1-gallon Ziploc freezer bag and submerge the sealed bag in the ice bath. Let stand, adding more ice as necessary, until cold, about 30 minutes.

FREEZE Remove the frozen canister from the freezer, assemble your ice cream machine, and turn it on. Pour the ice cream base into the canister, add the caraway oil, and spin until thick and creamy.
Pack the ice cream into a storage container, mixing in the pumpernickel gravel as you go. Press a sheet of parchment directly against the surface and seal with an airtight lid. Freeze in the coldest part of your freezer until firm, at least 4 hours.

Makes about 1 quart

- 2⅔ cups whole milk
- 1 tablespoon plus 2 teaspoons cornstarch
- 2 ounces (4 tablespoons) cream cheese, softened
- ⅛ teaspoon fine sea salt
- 1½ cups heavy cream
- ¾ cup sugar
- 2 tablespoons molasses
- 2 tablespoons light corn syrup
- 3 to 4 drops caraway essential oil
- ½ cup Pumpernickel Gravel (page 196)

HUMMINGBIRD CAKE ICE CREAM

Banana, cinnamon, and cream cheese ice cream with crumbled cake, pineapple syrup, and toasted pecans.

Hummingbird Cake is one of the great American cakes. It's from the South (but of course). Imagine a cake with bananas, pecans, pineapple, and cinnamon, all topped with sweet cream cheese frosting. When I first heard about it, it sounded like eight or nine church potluck desserts tossed together into some sort of Manna from Heaven Kitchen Sink Ambrosia Cake. But when you bite into it, all of the ingredients come together in a beautifully synergistic way.

Hummingbird Cake Ice Cream is like an inside-out Hummingbird Cake. The cream cheese ice cream serves as the carrier for the cake, pecans, banana, and pineapple syrup. To die for.

Makes about 1 quart

½ cup roughly crumbled Lady Cake (page 100), chilled

3 tablespoons Pineapple Sauce (page 184), chilled

2 tablespoons chopped toasted pecans

2⅔ cups whole milk

1 tablespoon plus 2 teaspoons cornstarch

5 ounces (10 tablespoons) cream cheese, softened

¼ teaspoon ground cinnamon

⅛ teaspoon fine sea salt

1½ cups heavy cream

¾ cup sugar

¼ cup light corn syrup

1 ripe banana

1 teaspoon vanilla extract

ADVANCE PREP Mix the cake, pineapple sauce, and pecans in a large bowl and freeze to use later.

PREP Mix about 2 tablespoons of the milk with the cornstarch in a small bowl to make a smooth slurry.

Whisk the cream cheese, cinnamon, and salt in a medium bowl until smooth.

Fill a large bowl with ice and water.

COOK Combine the remaining milk, the cream, sugar, and corn syrup in a 4-quart saucepan, bring to a boil over medium-high heat, and boil for 4 minutes. Remove from the heat and gradually whisk in the cornstarch slurry. Bring back to a boil over medium-high heat and cook, stirring with a heatproof spatula, until slightly thickened, about 1 minute. Remove from the heat.

CHILL Gradually whisk the hot milk mixture into the cream cheese until smooth.

Peel the banana, cut into chunks, and puree in a food processor until completely smooth. Stir the puree into the ice cream base and whisk in the vanilla extract. Pour the mixture into a 1-gallon Ziploc freezer bag and submerge the sealed bag in the ice bath. Let stand, adding more ice as necessary, until cold, about 30 minutes.

FREEZE Remove the frozen canister from the freezer, assemble your ice cream machine, and turn it on. Pour the ice cream base into the frozen canister and spin until thick and creamy.

Scoop the soft ice cream into the cake/pineapple sauce/pecan mixture and fold together until thoroughly combined—work quickly so the ice cream doesn't melt! Pack into a storage container. Press a sheet of parchment directly against the surface and seal with an airtight lid. Freeze in the coldest part of your freezer until firm, at least 4 hours.

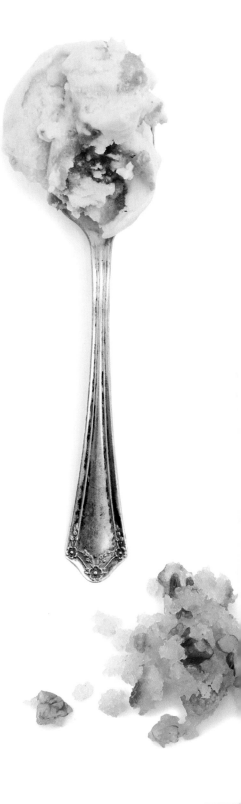

MANGO MANCHEGO ICE CREAM

Salty, creamy, nutty Manchego punctuated by velvety Mango Jam.

Manchego, a salty sheep's-milk cheese from Spain, makes a beautiful ice cream. You can use any version of the cheese, young or aged, here. The more aged the cheese is, the more nuttiness it has, but it is also harder, so it won't melt as easily. In that case, pour the hot milk mixture through a sieve.

Manchego is wonderful with our Mango Jam, or a combination we call Manguavo when we make it with our Guava Jam (page 182). This ice cream is even better when allowed to harden in the freezer. The nuttiness of the cheese blooms into the cream, and when frozen hard, the texture begins to mimic Manchego.

Makes about 1 quart

2⅔ cups whole milk

1 tablespoon plus 2 teaspoons cornstarch

2 ounces (4 tablespoons) cream cheese, softened

⅛ teaspoon fine sea salt

1½ cups heavy cream

¾ cup sugar

¼ cup light corn syrup

1 cup shredded Manchego

½ cup Mango Jam (page 182)

Parmesan Zucchini Lady Cake Ice Cream
When you have too many zucchini, try this. Replace the Manchego with a few good hunks of Parmesan rind. During the Chill step, strain out any large pieces. As you pack the ice cream into the storage container, layer in 2 cups of crumbled Zucchini Lady Cake (page 100) instead of the Mango Jam.

PREP Mix about 2 tablespoons of the milk with the cornstarch in a small bowl to make a smooth slurry.

Whisk the cream cheese and salt in a medium bowl until smooth.

Fill a large bowl with ice and water.

COOK Combine the remaining milk, the cream, sugar, and corn syrup in a 4-quart saucepan, bring to a boil over medium-high heat, and boil for 4 minutes. Remove from the heat and gradually whisk in the cornstarch slurry and Manchego. Bring the mixture back to a boil over medium-high heat and cook, stirring with a heatproof spatula, until slightly thickened, about 1 minute. Remove from the heat.

CHILL Gradually whisk the hot milk mixture into the cream cheese until smooth. Pour the mixture into a 1-gallon Ziploc freezer bag and submerge the sealed bag in the ice bath. Let stand, adding more ice as necessary, until cold, about 30 minutes.

FREEZE Remove the frozen canister from the freezer, assemble your ice cream machine, and turn it on. Pour the ice cream base into the canister and spin until thick and creamy.

Pack the ice cream into a storage container, layering in the jam as you go. Press a sheet of parchment directly against the surface and seal with an airtight lid. Freeze in the coldest part of your freezer until firm, at least 4 hours.

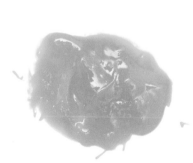

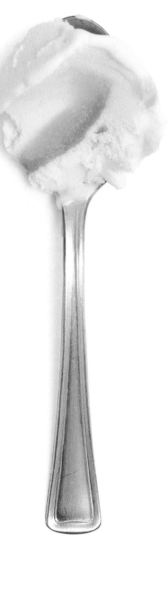

MANGO MANCHEGO ICE CREAM

MOONSHINE & CORN SYRUP CUSTARD WITH PECANS ICE CREAM

Full-bodied and smashingly distinct, with toasted salted pecans, gooey Corn Syrup Custard, and throat-warming moonshine.

I like the word *moonshine*. It's historic, dangerous, and illegal—all things that appeal to me (on some days). Moonshine is nothing more than white whiskey (young whiskey without the oak barrel aging). These days, the white whiskeys that micro-distillers are making are of very high quality and are quite far from what anyone would ever refer to as moonshine. Still, who can resist using the word *moonshine*? It just gives the whole thing more personality.

Moonshine, distilled from corn, is the perfect complement to Corn Syrup Custard, which is made with, you guessed it, corn syrup—itself a sort of food world outlaw. These two together are a dangerous and deadly delicious combination.

Makes about 1 quart

2⅔ cups whole milk

1 tablespoon plus 2 teaspoons cornstarch

2 ounces (4 tablespoons) cream cheese, softened

⅛ teaspoon fine sea salt

1½ cups heavy cream

⅔ cup sugar

¼ cup light corn syrup

⅓ to ½ cup moonshine or white whiskey (see Sources, page 200)

⅔ cup toasted salted pecan halves

½ cup Corn Syrup Custard (page 183)

KINGS COUNTY DISTILLERY
moonshine
corn whiskey 200ml
40% alcohol by volume

PREP Mix about 2 tablespoons of the milk with the cornstarch in a small bowl to make a smooth slurry.

Whisk the cream cheese and salt in a medium bowl until smooth.

Fill a large bowl with ice and water.

COOK Combine the remaining milk, the cream, sugar, and corn syrup in a 4-quart saucepan, bring to a boil over medium-high heat, and boil for 4 minutes. Remove from the heat and gradually whisk in the cornstarch slurry. Bring the mixture back to a boil over medium-high heat and cook, stirring with a heatproof spatula, until slightly thickened, about 1 minute. Remove from the heat.

CHILL Gradually whisk the hot milk mixture into the cream cheese until smooth. Pour the mixture into a 1-gallon Ziploc freezer bag and submerge the sealed bag in the ice bath. Let stand, adding more ice as necessary, until cold, about 30 minutes. Stir in the moonshine.

FREEZE Remove the frozen canister from the freezer, assemble your ice cream machine, and turn it on. Pour the ice cream base into the canister and spin until thick and creamy.

Pack the ice cream into a storage container, layering in the pecans and custard as you go. Press a sheet of parchment directly against the surface and seal with an airtight lid. Freeze in the coldest part of your freezer until firm, at least 4 hours.

WHITE HOUSE CHERRY ICE CREAM

Cherry-blossom-scented cream, white chocolate flecks, and sugar-plumped cherries.

White House Cherry has been an American ice cream flavor since the 1920s. The origin of the name is unclear, but perhaps it is an homage to the classic story of George Washington cutting down the cherry tree. The name is far better than the flavor of most versions, which had not even a whiff of vanilla, just cream whipped with loads of air and a smattering of maraschino cherries, which bear no resemblance to fresh cherries or the cherry blossom trees that bloom near the White House.

Simply put, White House Cherry was screaming for re-invention. My version is flavored with cherry blossom extract, which tastes like almonds and plums and has an intriguing salty scent (think sea breezes). We spin very fine threads of white chocolate into it to boost the creaminess. And then there are the cherries. Ours are dried and then sugar-plumped and taste exactly like what they are: real cherries.

Sometimes I also add handfuls of bright green salted pistachios. The result is almost a new take on Spumoni. And, it makes a nice ice cream to freeze into a sliceable terrine loaf at the holidays. Serve with crumbled meringues (see page 102) as a garnish.

Makes about 1 quart

- 2⅔ cups whole milk
- 1 tablespoon plus 2 teaspoons cornstarch
- 2 ounces (4 tablespoons) cream cheese, softened
- ⅛ teaspoon fine sea salt
- 1½ cups heavy cream
- ¾ cup sugar
- ¼ cup light corn syrup
- 1 to 2 drops cherry blossom extract
- 4 ounces white chocolate, chopped
- ¼ cup White House Cherries (page 186), drained
- A handful of pistachios (optional)

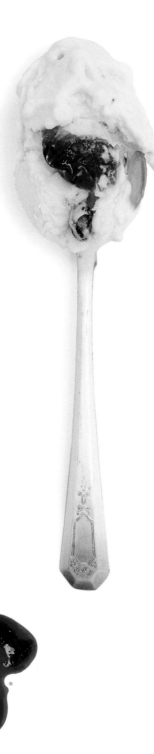

PREP Mix about 2 tablespoons of the milk with the cornstarch in a small bowl to make a smooth slurry.

Whisk the cream cheese and salt in a medium bowl until smooth. Fill a large bowl with ice and water.

COOK Combine the remaining milk, the cream, sugar, and corn syrup in a 4-quart saucepan, bring to a boil over medium-high heat, and boil for 4 minutes. Remove from the heat and gradually whisk in the cornstarch slurry. Bring the mixture back to a boil over medium-high heat and cook, stirring with a heatproof spatula, until slightly thickened, about 1 minute. Remove from the heat.

CHILL Gradually whisk the hot milk mixture into the cream cheese until smooth. Pour the mixture into a 1-gallon Ziploc freezer bag and submerge the sealed bag in the ice bath. Let stand, adding more ice as necessary, until cold, about 30 minutes.

FREEZE Remove the frozen canister from the freezer, assemble your ice cream machine, and turn it on. Pour the ice cream base into the canister, add the cherry blossom extract, and spin until thick and creamy. Meanwhile, melt the chocolate in a double boiler over simmering water. Remove from the heat and let cool until tepid but still pourable.

When the ice cream is almost ready, gradually drizzle the melted chocolate through the opening in the top of the machine and allow it to solidify and then break up in the ice cream for about 2 minutes.

Pack the ice cream into a storage container, folding in the cherries and pistachios, if using, as you go. Press a sheet of parchment directly against the surface and seal with an airtight lid. Freeze in the coldest part of your freezer until firm, at least 4 hours.

YAZOO SUE ICE CREAM WITH ROSEMARY BAR NUTS

Creamy cherry-wood-smoked porter with savory "bar nuts" dusted with rosemary, brown sugar, and cayenne.

We love to work with like-minded people from the world of food and drink, which is why we are friends with Linus and Lila at Yazoo Brewing Company. Yazoo, just a few miles from our East Nashville scoop shop, is responsible for the wonderful Yazoo Sue, the handcrafted porter that fuels this special ice cream. The first time I tried the beer, I fell in love with it. It's 9-percent alcohol and it packs a wallop. Rich, creamy, and smoky, the beer tastes meaty, in a good way.

As I wondered about what to pair it with, I thought of the herbs and spices you might make into a rub for smoking meats. So, we gathered every nut that we stock in our kitchen, coated them in rosemary, brown sugar, salt, and cayenne, and baked them. The result quickly became one of our most beloved year-round flavors.

Makes about 1 quart

2⅔ cups whole milk

1 tablespoon plus 2 teaspoons cornstarch

2 ounces (4 tablespoons) cream cheese, softened

⅛ teaspoon fine sea salt

1½ cups heavy cream

¾ cup sugar

¼ cup light corn syrup

⅓ cup smoked porter, preferably Yazoo Sue cherry wood (see Sources, page 200)

½ cup Rosemary Bar Nuts (page 192)

PREP Mix about 2 tablespoons of the milk with the cornstarch in a small bowl to make a smooth slurry.

Whisk the cream cheese and salt in a medium bowl until smooth. Fill a large bowl with ice and water.

COOK Combine the remaining milk, the cream, sugar, and corn syrup in a 4-quart saucepan, bring to a boil over medium-high heat, and boil for 4 minutes. Remove from the heat and gradually whisk in the cornstarch slurry. Bring the mixture back to a boil over medium-high heat and cook, stirring with a heatproof spatula, until slightly thickened, about 1 minute. Remove from the heat.

CHILL Gradually whisk the hot milk mixture into the cream cheese until smooth, then stir in the beer. Pour the mixture into a 1-gallon Ziploc freezer bag and submerge the sealed bag in the ice bath. Let stand, adding more ice as necessary, until cold, about 30 minutes.

FREEZE Remove the frozen canister from the freezer, assemble your ice cream machine, and turn it on. Pour the ice cream base into the canister and spin until thick and creamy.

Pack the ice cream into a storage container, folding in the bar nuts as you go. Press a sheet of parchment directly against the surface, and seal with an airtight lid. Freeze in the coldest part of your freezer until firm, at least 4 hours.

SALTY VANILLA FROZEN CUSTARD

Like pastry cream from a lovely bakery—rich, creamy, with a subtle saltiness.

Everywhere you look lately, it's salty in the sweets department. I'm not talking about traditional salted caramels from France, but slightly saltier versions of sweets, like our Salty Caramel and other flavors like our Mango Manchego Ice Cream (page 52).

Salty custard, though, is not really a part of that trend. It is a traditional flavor from Columbus, Ohio—I just made it into an ice cream. It's what makes the cream puffs at Schmidt's Sausage Haus in German Village so very craveable. They are filled with a custard that, whether originally intended to be or not, is salty. And it's rich, eggy, and creamy. This custard version of it is great on its own or stuffed into Cream Puffs (page 130).

This recipe can be used as a base for other frozen custards—simply omit the vanilla extract and reduce the salt to ½ teaspoon.

Makes about 1 quart

2¾ cups whole milk

6 large egg yolks

1 tablespoon plus 2 teaspoons cornstarch

1 ounce (2 tablespoons) cream cheese, softened

¾ teaspoon fine sea salt

3 teaspoons vanilla extract

1 cup heavy cream

¾ cup sugar

2 tablespoons light corn syrup

Salty Goat's-Milk Chocolate Frozen Custard
In the Cook step, reduce whole milk to 2 cups and add ¾ cup evaporated goat's milk (see Sources, page 200) to the saucepan with the cream, sugar, and corn syrup. After you cook the egg yolks, add 2 ounces bittersweet chocolate (70% or more cacao) and stir until completely melted.

PREP Mix about 2 tablespoons of the milk, the egg yolks, and cornstarch in a small bowl and set aside.

Whisk the cream cheese, salt, and vanilla in a medium bowl until smooth.

Fill a large bowl with ice and water.

COOK Combine the remaining milk, the cream, sugar, and corn syrup in a 4-quart saucepan, bring to a boil over medium-high heat, and boil for 4 minutes. Remove from the heat and gradually add about 2 cups of the hot milk mixture to the egg yolk mixture, one ladleful at a time, stirring well after each addition. Pour the mixture back into the saucepan and heat over medium heat, stirring constantly with a heatproof spatula, just until the mixture comes to a boil. Remove from the heat and strain through a sieve if necessary.

CHILL Gradually whisk the hot milk mixture into the cream cheese mixture until smooth. Pour the mixture into a 1-gallon Ziploc freezer bag and submerge the sealed bag in the ice bath. Let stand, adding more ice as necessary, until cold, about 30 minutes.

FREEZE Remove the frozen canister from the freezer, assemble your ice cream machine, and turn it on. Pour the custard base into the canister and spin until thick and creamy.

Pack the custard into a storage container. Press a sheet of parchment directly against the surface and seal with an airtight lid. Freeze in the coldest part of your freezer until firm, at least 4 hours.

Rum Plum Frozen Custard
In the Prep step, add 2 teaspoons vanilla extract to the cream cheese. In the Chill step, stir in ¼ cup spiced rum before you chill the mixture in the ice bath. In the Freeze step, fold in ⅓ cup roughly chopped Rum-Plumped Prunes (page 185) as you pack the ice cream into the storage container.

FRENCH TOAST FROZEN CUSTARD

A red-hot cinnamon-flavored maple frozen custard. Breakfast in a bite.

One of my favorite breakfast treats has also been one of our most-loved flavors over the years. It's so simple. The toasted bread gradually turns into cake if you let it bloom in the frozen custard for a few days in the freezer. If you happen to have a couple of pieces of brioche lying around, use them. But there is no need to go out and purchase a whole new loaf—you can use any bread you've got on hand.

You can also enjoy this as a simple Maple Frozen Custard by omitting the cinnamon, coffee, and brioche.

Makes about 1 quart

2¾ cups whole milk

6 large egg yolks

1 tablespoon plus 2 teaspoons cornstarch

1 ounce (2 tablespoons) cream cheese, softened

½ teaspoon vanilla extract

1 teaspoon ground cinnamon

1 teaspoon freshly roasted, finely ground coffee

¼ teaspoon salt

1 cup heavy cream

2 tablespoons light corn syrup

1½ cups maple syrup

½ cup (¼-inch) brioche cubes (from 2 to 3 slices brioche), toasted, or French Toast Gravel (page 197)

PREP Mix about 2 tablespoons of the milk, the egg yolks, and cornstarch in a small bowl and set aside.

Whisk the cream cheese, vanilla, cinnamon, coffee, and salt in a medium bowl until smooth.

Mix the cream with the corn syrup in a small bowl.

Fill a large bowl with ice and water.

COOK Bring the maple syrup to a boil in a 4-quart saucepan over medium-high heat. Reduce the heat to medium and continue cooking for 8 minutes, until the syrup has reduced by half. Remove from the heat and gradually add the cream mixture, one ladleful at a time, stirring constantly. Stir in the remaining milk. Return the saucepan to the stovetop and heat over medium heat, bringing the mixture to a rolling boil, and cook for 4 minutes (it may appear curdled from the acidic maple, but it will come back together in the finished custard). Remove from the heat and gradually add about 2 cups of this mixture to the egg yolk mixture, one ladleful at a time, stirring well after each addition.

Pour the mixture into the saucepan and heat over medium heat until the mixture returns to a boil, then remove from the heat. Strain through a sieve if necessary.

CHILL Gradually whisk the hot milk mixture into the cream cheese mixture until smooth. Pour the mixture into a 1-gallon Ziploc freezer bag and submerge the sealed bag in the ice bath. Let stand, adding more ice as necessary, until cold, about 30 minutes.

FREEZE Remove the frozen canister from the freezer, assemble your ice cream machine, and turn it on. Pour the custard base into the canister, and spin until thick and creamy.

Pack the custard into a storage container, mixing in the toasted brioche cubes as you go. Press a sheet of parchment directly against the surface and seal with an airtight lid. Freeze in the coldest part of your freezer until firm, at least 4 hours.

FRENCH TOAST FROZEN CUSTARD

MIDDLE WEST EGGNOG FROZEN CUSTARD

Velvety custard flavor, with notes of vanilla and caramel spiked with whiskey.

My grandfather James Britton made his eggnog with whiskey, and plenty of it; I like it better than rum or brandy versions. Whiskey can be more bracing and gives the eggnog some grit. It's boozy, totally Midwestern, warm, spirited, and celebratory. This frozen custard has been on our holiday list for as long as I can remember.

As we are wont to do at Jeni's, we use an Ohio red wheat whiskey, distilled by our friends at Middle West Spirits. They also distill an incredible bourbon.

Makes about 1 quart

2¾ cups whole milk

6 large egg yolks

1 tablespoon plus 2 teaspoons cornstarch

1 ounce (2 tablespoons) cream cheese, softened

½ teaspoon fine sea salt

⅛ teaspoon grated nutmeg

½ teaspoon vanilla extract

1 cup heavy cream

¾ cup sugar

2 tablespoons light corn syrup

¼ cup whiskey (or rum or brandy)

PREP Mix about 2 tablespoons of the milk, the egg yolks, and cornstarch in a small bowl and set aside.

Whisk the cream cheese, salt, nutmeg, and vanilla in a medium bowl until smooth.

Fill a large bowl with ice and water.

COOK Combine the remaining milk, the cream, sugar, and corn syrup in a 4-quart saucepan, bring to a boil over medium-high heat, and boil for 4 minutes. Remove from the heat and gradually add about 2 cups of the hot milk mixture to the egg yolk mixture, one ladleful at a time, stirring well after each addition. Pour the mixture back into the saucepan and heat over medium heat, stirring constantly with a heatproof spatula, just until the mixture comes to a boil. Remove from the heat and strain through a sieve if necessary.

CHILL Gradually whisk the hot milk mixture into the cream cheese mixture until smooth. Pour the mixture into a 1-gallon Ziploc freezer bag and submerge the sealed bag in the ice bath. Let stand, adding more ice as necessary, until cold, about 30 minutes.

FREEZE Remove the frozen canister from the freezer, assemble your ice cream machine, and turn it on. Pour the custard base into the canister, add the whiskey, and spin until thick and creamy.

Pack the custard into a storage container. Press a sheet of parchment directly against the surface and seal with an airtight lid. Freeze in the coldest part of your freezer until firm, at least 4 hours.

ORANGE-BLOSSOM BISQUE TORTONI FROZEN CUSTARD

Rich frozen custard scented with orange flowers,
studded with toasted almonds and crumbled amaretti.

This flavor tastes like it got into a time machine a hundred years ago and landed in your kitchen. When you taste it, it will have the reverse effect, sending you back in time—to when women were doused in floral waters and pastries were soused with them.

Traditionally Bisque Tortoni Ice Cream is served in paper soufflé cups with a cherry on top. Amarena cherries would be perfect here.

Makes about 1 quart

2¾ cups whole milk

6 large egg yolks

1 tablespoon plus 2 teaspoons cornstarch

1 ounce (2 tablespoons) cream cheese, softened

2 teaspoons vanilla extract

¾ teaspoon almond extract

½ teaspoon fine sea salt

1 cup heavy cream

¾ cup sugar

2 tablespoons light corn syrup

1 to 2 drops neroli essential oil or 1 teaspoon orange flower water (see Sources, page 200)

½ cup toasted almonds, very finely chopped

½ cup crumbled amaretti cookies

12 to 16 Amarena cherries (see Sources, page 200; optional)

PREP Mix about 2 tablespoons of the milk, the egg yolks, and cornstarch in a small bowl and set aside.

Whisk the cream cheese, vanilla, almond extract, and salt in a medium bowl until smooth.

Fill a large bowl with ice and water.

COOK Combine the remaining milk, the cream, sugar, and corn syrup in a 4-quart saucepan, bring to a boil over medium-high heat, and boil for 4 minutes. Remove from the heat and gradually add about 2 cups of the hot milk mixture to the egg yolk mixture, one ladleful at a time, stirring well after each addition. Pour the mixture back into the saucepan and heat over medium heat, stirring constantly with a heatproof spatula, just until the mixture comes to a boil. Remove from the heat and strain through a sieve if necessary.

CHILL Gradually whisk the hot milk mixture into the cream cheese mixture until smooth. Pour the mixture into a 1-gallon Ziploc freezer bag and submerge the sealed bag in the ice bath. Let stand, adding more ice as necessary, until cold, about 30 minutes.

FREEZE Remove the frozen canister from the freezer, assemble your ice cream machine, and turn it on. Pour the custard base into the canister, drop the neroli essential oil into the top, and spin until thick and creamy.

Pack the custard into a storage container, layering in the toasted almonds and amaretti as you go. Press a sheet of parchment directly against the surface and seal with an airtight lid. Freeze in the coldest part of your freezer until firm, at least 4 hours.

Garnish with the cherries, if using, as you serve.

Note: There are two other ways to pack this custard for storing and serving.

Freezing on a baking sheet for slicing: Spread the custard out thinly on a 13-by-18-inch baking sheet. Top with the almonds and amaretti. Arrange the cherries, if using, in even rows of 3 or 4 across. Freeze for at least 4 hours. Serve by slicing into squares, with a cherry in the center of each one.

The traditional way: Spoon into paper soufflé cups. Top each one with some almonds and amaretti and a cherry. Freeze on a cookie sheet. Freeze these for a bit less than the other methods if you want slightly softer custard.

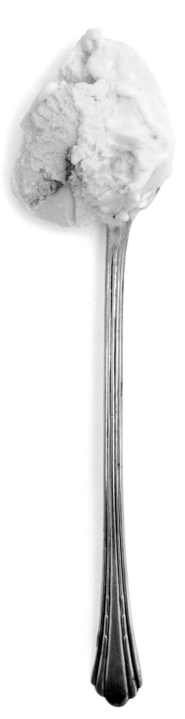

ORANGE-BLOSSOM BISQUE TORTONI FROZEN CUSTARD

BUTTERMILK SOFT-SERVE

A lighter, tangy ice cream with super-rich dairy flavors, served soft or hard.

This ice cream straddles the edge between lightness and richness. The buttermilk actually intensifies the creamy flavor and the light texture. (However, if you prefer, you can make this recipe with whole or 2% milk for a more traditional soft-serve.) It is really fun to freeze in one of the new soft-serve ice cream machines, but if you don't have one, you can just use a regular machine and serve it soft directly from the machine. You can also, of course, harden it like the other ice creams. It is delightful with the Stone-Ground-Grits Pudding Cake (page 106). And we completely freaked out over it with Peoria Corn Fritters (page 136) and any fruit sauce or fresh fruit. It also goes with any cake or pie in the book, whether soft or frozen hard.

Makes about 1 quart

1¼ cups heavy cream

2 tablespoons cornstarch

3 ounces (6 tablespoons) cream cheese, softened

¼ teaspoon fine sea salt

⅔ cup sugar

2 tablespoons light corn syrup

2½ cups buttermilk, whole milk, or 2% milk

PREP Mix 3 to 4 tablespoons of the cream with the cornstarch in a small bowl to make a smooth slurry.

Whisk the cream cheese and salt in a medium bowl until smooth. Fill a large bowl with ice and water.

COOK Combine the remaining cream, the sugar, and corn syrup in a 4-quart saucepan, bring to a boil over medium-high heat, and boil for 4 minutes. Remove from the heat and gradually whisk in the cornstarch slurry. Bring the mixture back to a boil over medium-high heat and cook, stirring with a heatproof spatula, until slightly thickened, about 20 seconds. Remove from the heat.

CHILL Gradually whisk the hot milk mixture into the cream cheese until smooth. Stir in the buttermilk.

Pour the mixture into a 1-gallon Ziploc bag and submerge the sealed bag in the ice bath. Let stand, adding more ice as necessary, until cold, about 30 minutes.

FREEZE

If using a soft-serve machine
Remove the frozen canister from the freezer, assemble your ice cream machine, and turn it on. Pour the ice cream base into the canister and spin until thick and creamy. Use the handle to release some of the ice cream into a bowl. If the ice cream is too soft, dump it back in and keep churning until it reaches the desired consistency. Serve immediately.

If using a regular ice cream machine
Remove the frozen canister from the freezer, assemble your ice cream machine, and turn it on. Pour the ice cream base into the canister and spin until thick and creamy.

Serve directly from the machine, or, for a scoopable version, pack the ice cream into a storage container. Press a sheet of parchment directly against the surface and seal with an airtight lid. Freeze in the coldest part of your freezer until firm, at least 4 hours.

D V

CRÈME SANS LAIT

For those among us who cannot, do not, or will not eat dairy . . . and everyone else too.

Our nondairy Crème sans Lait is fabulous. It would be phenomenal in J-Bars (page 166), coated with chocolate, or just as a sort of dairy-free pudding pop. We eat a lot of Crème sans Lait with Runny Chocolate Sauce (page 190) or Brrrr Sauce (page 186) on top and sliced bananas around the edges.

You can use this base recipe to make many flavors, but it works best with only minimal additions to the mixture before freezing. The texture gets really thrown off with the addition of something watery—say berries or beer—which causes it to turn a bit gritty and icy. But there are tons of other options for flavoring it using essential oils, concentrates, and extracts. And you can toss in crumbled cookies or cakes, or nuts. This recipe gets its richness from refined coconut oil (which does not taste like coconut) and pulverized cashews, and a little boost in flavor and texture from vegan cream cheese, although you can leave it out if you wish.

Makes about 1 quart

2¾ cups almond milk

2 tablespoons tapioca starch

½ cup raw cashews, or ⅓ cup store-bought cashew paste

2 ounces (4 tablespoons) vegan cream cheese, preferably Follow Your Heart (see Sources, page 200), softened (optional)

1¼ cups refined coconut oil, at room temperature

⅔ cup sugar

⅓ cup light corn syrup

1 vanilla bean, split, seeds scraped out, seeds and bean reserved

❶   ❷   ❸

PREP Mix about 2 tablespoons of the almond milk with the tapioca starch in a small bowl to make a smooth slurry.

If using raw cashews, pulverize them into a very fine paste in a food processor or with a mortar and pestle. Whip the vegan cream cheese, if using, coconut oil, and cashew paste in a bowl until smooth and creamy.

Fill a large bowl with ice and water.

COOK Combine the remaining almond milk, the sugar, corn syrup, and vanilla seeds and bean pod in a 4-quart saucepan and heat over medium-high heat until bubbling. Remove the pan from the heat, drizzle in the tapioca starch slurry, and stir well. Bring the mixture to a boil over medium-high heat, reduce to a simmer, and let simmer for 30 seconds until the mixture thickens slightly. Remove from the heat.

CHILL Gradually whisk the hot milk mixture into the cream cheese mixture, stirring until well incorporated. Remove the vanilla bean and pour the mixture into a blender. Blend on high for 3 minutes to homogenize. Then pour the mixture into a 1-gallon Ziploc bag and submerge the sealed bag in the ice bath. Let stand, adding more ice as necessary, until cold, about 30 minutes.

FREEZE Remove the frozen canister from the freezer, assemble your ice cream machine, and turn it on. Pour the crème base into the canister and spin until thick and creamy.

Pack the crème into a storage container. Press a sheet of parchment directly against the surface, and seal with an airtight lid. Freeze in the coldest part of your freezer until firm, at least 4 hours.

❶ Rose Water & Pistachio Crème sans Lait

Omit the vanilla bean. Add 1 to 2 teaspoons rose water to the cooled base and then add a handful of pistachios to the crème when it's finished churning.

❷ Peanut Butter & Chocolate Crème sans Lait

Omit the vanilla bean. Add ½ cup pulverized peanuts along with the cashew paste. Drizzle 4 to 6 ounces of lukewarm melted chocolate into the machine when the ice cream has finished churning.

❸ Banilla Crème sans Lait

Puree 2 ripe bananas and add them to the cooled base just before freezing.

❹ Chocolate Crème sans Lait

Omit the vanilla bean. Combine ¾ cup strong dark-roast coffee, ½ cup sugar, and ½ cup Dutch processed cocoa powder in a small saucepan and heat over medium-high heat, whisking, until the sugar is dissolved and the mixture is smooth. Remove from the heat, add 2 ounces unsweetened chocolate, and let sit for 5 minutes to melt it. Stir until the mixture is again smooth. In a bowl, add the warm chocolate mixture to the cream cheese, along with the coconut oil and cashew paste, and whisk until smooth and creamy. Proceed as directed.

SALTY CARAMEL CRÈME SANS LAIT

A flavor that I have made for twenty years reborn in dairy-free form. A very successful new addition to the family!

Since 1996, we've made Salty Caramel Ice Cream, which is the flavor that put us on the map.

When I first heard a French chef I worked with in the early 1990s say that the caramel in his hometown in Brittany was salty, I thought it must be like the salty black licorice from Scandinavia (which is really salty), not the softly salted caramels from Brittany that he was actually referring to. So I started making salty caramel ice cream that was extra salty, trying to mimic what I thought they did in France. Turns out I was wrong. In France they make a distinction between a caramel that is salted and one that is not. In America we do not—it's all subtly salted. What a fortunate mix-up. My extra salty ice cream was an immediate sensation. Customers lined up at our counter for it and began to order it by the case on our website. We still make it the same way, by caramelizing sugar in a kettle over fire. It's dangerous and difficult to get just right, but we wouldn't do it any other way.

The way I see it, it's one thing to not be able to eat ice cream. It's a whole other thing to not be able to eat our Salty Caramel ice cream. So here is a dairy-free version that does it justice.

PREP Mix about 2 tablespoons of the almond milk with the tapioca starch in a small bowl to make a smooth slurry. If using raw cashews, pulverize them into a very fine paste in a food processor or with a mortar and pestle. Whisk the cream cheese, if using, coconut oil, cashew paste, and salt in a bowl until smooth and creamy.

Pour the corn syrup into the remaining almond milk in a bowl.

Fill a large bowl with ice and water.

Makes about 1 quart

- 2¾ cups almond milk
- 2 tablespoons tapioca starch
- ⅓ cup raw cashews
- 2 ounces (4 tablespoons) vegan cream cheese, preferably Follow Your Heart (see Sources, page 200), softened (optional)
- 1¼ cups refined coconut oil, at room temperature
- ½ teaspoon fine sea salt
- ⅓ cup light corn syrup
- ⅔ cup sugar
- 1 vanilla bean, split, seeds scraped out, seeds and bean reserved

COOK Heat the sugar in a 4-quart saucepan over medium heat until it is melted and golden amber (see Note). Remove from the heat and, stirring constantly, slowly add a bit of the almond milk mixture to the caramel: it will fizzle, pop, and spurt. Stir until well combined, then add a little more almond milk and stir. Keep adding the milk a little at a time until it is all incorporated.

Slowly whisk in the tapioca starch slurry and the vanilla seeds and bean. Return the pan to the heat, bring to a boil over medium-high heat, and cook, stirring with a heatproof spatula, for 20 to 30 seconds, until the mixture thickens slightly. Remove from the heat. If any caramel flecks remain, strain the mixture through a sieve.

CHILL Gradually whisk the hot milk mixture into the cream cheese mixture, stirring until well incorporated. Pour the mixture into a 1-gallon Ziploc freezer bag and submerge the sealed bag in the ice bath. Let stand, adding more ice as necessary, until cold, about 30 minutes.

FREEZE Remove the frozen canister from the freezer, assemble your ice cream machine, and turn it on. Pour the crème base into the canister and spin until thick and creamy.

Remove the vanilla bean and discard. Pack the crème into a storage container. Press a sheet of parchment directly against the surface and seal with an airtight lid. Freeze in the coldest part of your freezer until firm, at least 4 hours.

Note: When making caramel, I use the dry-burn technique—I don't add water to the sugar before putting it over the heat, as some chefs do. Caramelizing sugar dry means it goes faster, but you have to watch it closely and be ready with your cream. Here is an overview of what you are going to do:

Stand over the pan of sugar with a heatproof spatula ready, but do not touch the sugar until there is a full layer of melted and browning liquid sugar on the bottom of the pan, with a smaller layer of unmelted sugar on top. When the edges of the melted sugar begin to darken, use the spatula to bring them into the center to help melt the unmelted sugar. Continue stirring and pushing the sugar around until it is all melted and evenly medium amber in color. Immediately but slowly pour about ¼ cup of the almond milk mixture into the burning-hot sugar. Be careful—it will pop and spit! Stir until it is incorporated, then add a bit more cream and stir, and continue until it has all been added.

FROZEN YOGURT BASE

Plain frozen yogurt, delightful on its own or flavored any way you like it.

I feel like I need to defend frozen yogurt here. "Fro-yo" has ruined the idea that frozen yogurt can be delicious. Astronaut-friendly, add-water fro-yo yogurt powder is not yogurt, no matter how many FDA standards it passes. At Jeni's, our frozen yogurt is made with biodynamic yogurt from Pennsylvania farms, as well as grass-fed milk and cream. Often it's made with fruit, since I find that the tartness of the yogurt always draws out and marries nicely with fruit.

Around the holidays, I make this recipe with whole milk yogurt instead of low-fat and add about a cup of sweetened chestnut paste to it. It's a lovely holiday offering. But you will never see flavors like chocolate, vanilla, or coffee yogurt at Jeni's. Even though chocolate and coffee can be acidic, the flavors clash with yogurt's natural flavors.

Makes about 1 quart

1 quart plain low-fat yogurt

1½ cups whole milk

2 tablespoons cornstarch

2 ounces (4 tablespoons) cream cheese, softened

⅔ cup heavy cream

⅔ cup sugar

⅓ cup light corn syrup

❶ Bergamot Frozen Yogurt

Make a bergamot syrup by combining ½ cup bergamot juice (or a mixture of half lemon juice and half lime juice) with 3 tablespoons sugar in a small saucepan. Bring to a boil over medium-high heat, stirring to dissolve the sugar. Let cool while you make the frozen yogurt base. In the Chill step, add the syrup to the base after adding the 1¼ cups yogurt. Proceed as directed.

❷ Huckleberry Frozen Yogurt

Make a huckleberry sauce by pureeing 1 cup fresh or frozen huckleberries (see Sources, page 200) in a food processor. Combine ½ cup of the puree (reserve the rest for another use) with ¼ cup sugar and 3 tablespoons lemon juice in a small saucepan. Bring to a boil over medium-high heat, stirring to dissolve the sugar. Let cool while you make the frozen yogurt base. In the Chill step, add the sauce to the base after adding the 1¼ cups yogurt. Proceed as directed.

ADVANCE PREP

For the strained yogurt

Set a sieve over a bowl and line it with two layers of cheesecloth. Pour the yogurt into the sieve, cover with plastic wrap, and refrigerate for 6 to 8 hours to drain. Discard the liquid and measure out 1¼ cups strained yogurt; set aside (see The Quick Take, page 16).

PREP Mix about 2 tablespoons of the milk with the cornstarch in a small bowl to make a smooth slurry.

Whisk the cream cheese in a medium bowl until smooth.

Fill a large bowl with ice and water.

COOK Combine the remaining milk, the cream, sugar, and corn syrup in a 4-quart saucepan, bring to a boil over medium-high heat, and boil for 4 minutes. Remove from the heat and gradually whisk in the cornstarch slurry. Bring the mixture back to a boil over medium-high heat and cook, stirring with a heatproof spatula, until slightly thickened, about 1 minute. Remove from the heat.

CHILL Gradually whisk the hot milk mixture into the cream cheese until smooth. Add the reserved 1¼ cups yogurt. Pour the mixture into a 1-gallon Ziploc freezer bag and submerge the sealed bag in the ice bath. Let stand, adding more ice as necessary, until cold, about 30 minutes.

FREEZE Remove the frozen canister from the freezer, assemble your ice cream machine, and turn it on. Pour the frozen yogurt base into the frozen canister and spin until thick and creamy.

Pack the frozen yogurt into a storage container. Press a sheet of parchment directly against the surface and seal with an airtight lid. Freeze in the coldest part of your freezer until firm, at least 4 hours.

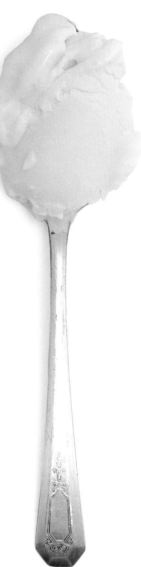

❸ Mango Lassi Frozen Yogurt

Make a mango sauce by combining 1 cup sweetened mango pulp (see Sources, page 200) or ⅔ cup mango puree (from 2 to 3 mangoes) with ¼ cup sugar in a small saucepan. Bring to a boil over medium-high heat, stirring to dissolve the sugar. Let cool while you make the frozen yogurt base. In the Chill step, add the sauce to the base after adding the 1 ¼ cups yogurt. Proceed as directed.

FRESH GINGER FROZEN YOGURT

*Astringent lemon yogurt scented with fresh ginger
and made colorful with beets and turmeric.*

I love ginger. The combination of ginger and lemon is one
of my favorites, and this frozen yogurt is for all ginger
lovers. Yogurt is actually a much better pairing with ginger
than straight cream, because the tartness offsets it and
draws attention to it. It is also lighter in body. We add beet
powder and turmeric to make it the color of Japanese
pickled ginger.

ADVANCE PREP

For the strained yogurt

Set a sieve over a bowl and line it with two layers of cheesecloth. Pour
the yogurt into the sieve, cover with plastic wrap, and refrigerate for
6 to 8 hours to drain. Discard the liquid and measure out 1¼ cups
strained yogurt; set aside.

PREP

For the ginger syrup

Combine the lemon juice with the sugar in a small saucepan and bring
to a boil over medium-high heat, stirring to dissolve the sugar. Remove
from the heat, add the sliced ginger and powdered ginger, and let cool.
Strain out the sliced ginger and set the syrup aside.

For the frozen yogurt base

Mix about 2 tablespoons of the milk with the cornstarch in a small bowl
to make a smooth slurry.

    Whisk the cream cheese, beet powder, and turmeric, if using, in a
medium bowl until smooth.

    Fill a large bowl with ice and water.

Makes about 1 quart

FROZEN YOGURT BASE

1 quart plain low-fat yogurt

1½ cups whole milk

2 tablespoons cornstarch

2 ounces (4 tablespoons)
   cream cheese, softened

½ teaspoon beet powder (for color;
   see Sources, page 200; optional)

⅛ teaspoon turmeric (for color;
   optional)

½ cup heavy cream

⅔ cup sugar

¼ cup light corn syrup

GINGER SYRUP

½ cup fresh lemon juice
   (from 2 to 3 lemons)

3 tablespoons sugar

2 ounces fresh ginger
   (a piece about 4 inches long),
   peeled and sliced into ⅛-inch coins

½ teaspoon powdered ginger

COOK Combine the remaining milk, the cream, sugar, and corn syrup in a 4-quart saucepan, bring to a boil over medium-high heat, and boil for 4 minutes. Remove from the heat and gradually whisk in the cornstarch slurry. Bring the mixture back to a boil over medium-high heat and cook, stirring with a heatproof spatula, until slightly thickened, about 1 minute. Remove from the heat.

CHILL Gradually whisk the hot milk mixture into the cream cheese until smooth. Add the 1¼ cups yogurt and the ginger syrup. Pour the mixture into a 1-gallon Ziploc freezer bag and submerge the sealed bag in the ice bath. Let stand, adding more ice as necessary, until cold, about 30 minutes.

FREEZE Remove the frozen canister from the freezer, assemble your ice cream machine, and turn it on. Pour the frozen yogurt base into the frozen canister and spin until thick and creamy.

Pack the frozen yogurt into a storage container. Press a sheet of parchment directly against the surface and seal with an airtight lid. Freeze in the coldest part of your freezer until firm, at least 4 hours.

FRESH PEACH FROZEN YOGURT

When peaches are at their peak, this flavor sings.
Yogurt highlights the peaches' natural tartness.

Our friends Stephen and Jessica Rose own The Peach Truck in Nashville. Every week during peach season, Stephen—part of this fifth-generation peach-farming family from Georgia—hand-picks the best peaches from his family's farm. He and Jessica then haul them to Nashville, where customers who have preordered the beautiful peaches pick them up from the bed of Stephen and Jessica's Peach Truck, a dark green 1964 Jeep Gladiator.

When you meet Stephen and Jessica to claim your peaches, you always have a Nashville moment. The wind blows just so and seems to sing a lilting tune. Chirping bluebirds fly overhead. Someone plays a fiddle barely within earshot. Even though office buildings are part of the landscape, you'll swear you hear the cozy sound of a screen door shutting in the distance. And every conversation will stretch and linger.

After chatting with Stephen and Jessica—and no doubt the new friends you invariably make—you bid everyone farewell, climb into your car, roll the windows down, and drive away with a smile, peach juice dripping down your chin, and begin looking forward to next week's delivery.

Makes about 1 quart

FROZEN YOGURT BASE

1 quart plain low-fat yogurt

⅔ cup buttermilk
  (or additional whole milk)

1 cup whole milk

2 tablespoons cornstarch

2 ounces (4 tablespoons)
  cream cheese, softened

¼ teaspoon fine sea salt

½ cup heavy cream

⅔ cup sugar

¼ cup light corn syrup

PEACH PUREE

2 to 3 ripe golden peaches, peeled,
  pitted, and cut into rough chunks

⅓ cup sugar

¼ cup fresh lemon juice
  (from about 2 lemons)

ADVANCE PREP

For the strained yogurt

Set a sieve over a bowl and line it with two layers of cheesecloth. Pour the yogurt into the sieve, cover with plastic wrap, and refrigerate for 6 to 8 hours to drain. Discard the liquid and measure out 1¼ cups strained yogurt. Add the buttermilk and set aside.

PREP

For the frozen yogurt

Mix about 2 tablespoons of the milk with the cornstarch in a small bowl to make a smooth slurry.

Whisk the cream cheese and salt in a medium bowl until smooth.

Fill a large bowl with ice and water.

For the peach puree

Puree the peaches in a food processor. Transfer ⅔ cup of the puree to a small bowl. Reserve the rest for another use.

Combine the sugar and lemon juice in a medium saucepan and bring to a boil over medium-high heat, stirring until the sugar dissolves. Add to the peach puree and let cool.

COOK Combine the remaining milk, the cream, sugar, and corn syrup in a 4-quart saucepan, bring to a boil over medium-high heat, and boil for 4 minutes. Remove from the heat and gradually whisk in the cornstarch slurry. Bring the mixture back to a boil over medium-high heat and cook, stirring with a heatproof spatula, until slightly thickened, about 1 minute. Remove from the heat.

CHILL Gradually whisk the hot milk mixture into the cream cheese until smooth. Add the reserved 1¼ cups yogurt and the peach puree. Pour the mixture into a 1-gallon Ziploc freezer bag and submerge the sealed bag in the ice bath. Let stand, adding more ice as necessary, until cold, about 30 minutes.

FREEZE Remove the frozen canister from the freezer, assemble your ice cream machine, and turn it on. Pour the frozen yogurt base into the frozen canister and spin until thick and creamy.

Pack the frozen yogurt into a storage container. Press a sheet of parchment directly against the surface and seal with an airtight lid. Freeze in the coldest part of your freezer until firm, at least 4 hours.

ICELANDIC HAPPY MARRIAGE CAKE FROZEN SKYR

Tangy skyr with cubes of Lady Cake, Oat Streusel, and Stewed Rhubarb Sauce.

Skyr is a fat-free yogurt-like product from Iceland. Since everything from Iceland is magical and wondrous, we knew that an ice cream made with skyr would be too. Siggi's is a brand that you can get almost everywhere now, and we love to use it for this. I'm in favor of well-made products that people put their real names on.

This flavor, along with Magnolia Mochi Ice Cream (page 45), was originally part of our Super Pop Cakes collection. Since we love the pop music hailing from Iceland, we had to have a cake from there, too. Icelandic Happy Marriage Cake is a traditional cake that was irresistible. So we retooled it into a frozen yogurt . . . um, skyr.

Makes about 1 quart

1½ cups whole milk

2 tablespoons cornstarch

1¼ cups skyr (see headnote)

2 ounces (4 tablespoons) cream cheese, softened

½ cup heavy cream

⅔ cup sugar

¼ cup light corn syrup

½ cup crumbled Lady Cake (page 100), frozen

½ cup Streusel (page 120), made with oats and baked an additional 20 minutes

⅔ cup Stewed Rhubarb Sauce (page 185)

PREP Mix about 2 tablespoons of the milk with the cornstarch in a small bowl to make a smooth slurry.

Whisk the skyr and cream cheese in a medium bowl until smooth. Fill a large bowl with ice and water.

COOK Combine the remaining milk, the cream, sugar, and corn syrup in a 4-quart saucepan, bring to a boil over medium-high heat, and boil for 4 minutes. Remove from the heat and gradually whisk in the cornstarch slurry. Bring the mixture back to a boil over medium-high heat and cook, stirring with a heatproof spatula, until slightly thickened, about 1 minute. Remove from the heat.

CHILL Gradually whisk the hot milk mixture into the cream cheese until smooth. Pour the mixture into a 1-gallon Ziploc freezer bag and submerge the sealed bag in the ice bath. Let stand, adding more ice as necessary, until cold, about 30 minutes.

FREEZE Remove the frozen canister from the freezer, assemble your ice cream machine, and turn it on. Pour the yogurt base into the canister and spin until thick and creamy.

Working quickly, pack the frozen yogurt into a storage container, alternating layers of frozen yogurt, cake, streusel, and rhubarb sauce. Press a sheet of parchment directly against the surface and seal with an airtight lid. Freeze in the coldest part of your freezer until firm, at least 4 hours.

RAINBOW FROZEN YOGURT

Light and pretty, three tasty yogurts come together on your tongue.

Rainbowing ice cream means to combine two or three different flavors into one container so that when you run the scoop through the ice cream, you pick up all three flavors. One of our most popular variations is our Rainbow Frozen Yogurt, which is always a hit with everyone, especially children. We make the frozen yogurt with a variety of different colors, traditionally during Pride Week in Columbus.

This is a particularly smashing combination of tastes, aromas, and visuals—Ginger, Huckleberry, and Mango—but you can choose any flavors you wish.

Makes about 3 quarts

Fresh Ginger Frozen Yogurt
(page 76)

Huckleberry Frozen Yogurt
(page 74)

Mango Lassi Frozen Yogurt
(page 75)

In our kitchen, we call this the Monkey Bread Technique. The trick is to distribute all of the flavors evenly so that each container (and each scoop) gets an even swirl of them all. If you've ever made monkey bread, this is a similar assembly technique—layering three flavors in equal-size globs, one on top of the other.

Using the same method, we do blends of ice creams and sorbets and sometimes add other textural elements to make, say, an Eton Mess Ice Cream composed of Sweet Cream Ice Cream, Red Raspberry Sorbet, and crushed meringues all in one flavor.

PREP Have 3 quart or 6 pint containers ready for action. Stage the frozen yogurts: remove them from the freezer and place them on the counter for about 10 minutes. They should still be frozen but slightly softened. Then, working quickly (I use a 4 ounce scoop, but you can experiment and use any size scoop you wish), layer balls of each frozen yogurt into your empty containers, moving from one flavor to another and back around again until you have used up all of the frozen yogurts.

FREEZE When you've finished scooping the yogurts into the containers, press a piece of parchment directly against the surface of each and seal with an airtight lid. Freeze in the coldest part of your freezer until firm, at least 4 hours.

BELLINI SORBET

Full of sunny, just-picked peaches and bright, unoaked white wine to mimic the famous cocktail.

This sorbet requires the fragrance of the ripest peaches. When they are available in your area, buy them and freeze them for making the sorbet later. We add just a little light, crisp white wine to give it the flavor of the Bellini, that ultimate summer cocktail. We use a white Burgundy, or a Soave, an unoaked white from northern Italy, instead of the traditional Prosecco, because the fizz is churned out during the freezing process, and even an excellent Prosecco or Champagne is ruined once the bubbles disappear.

As for the peaches, the classic recipe calls for white ones, but I have never found white peaches that taste as good as ripe yellow peaches. Maybe white peaches have changed since the Bellini was invented in 1934 in Venice, or maybe good white peaches just aren't available in Ohio.

COOK Combine the pureed peaches, sugar, corn syrup, wine, and lemon juice in a medium saucepan and bring to a boil, stirring until the sugar is dissolved. Transfer to a medium bowl and let cool.

CHILL Place the sorbet base in the refrigerator and chill for at least 2 hours.

FREEZE Remove the frozen canister from the freezer, assemble your ice cream machine, and turn it on. Pour the sorbet base into the canister and spin just until it is the consistency of very softly whipped cream.

Pack the sorbet into a storage container. Press a sheet of parchment directly against the surface and seal with an airtight lid. Freeze in the coldest part of your freezer until firm, at least 4 hours.

Makes about 1 quart

4 ripe peaches (about 1¾ pounds), peeled, pitted, and pureed in a food processor

⅔ cup sugar

¼ cup light corn syrup

⅔ cup white Burgundy or Soave

3 tablespoons fresh lemon juice

GRAPEFRUIT SORBET

Refreshing, bittersweet, and icy in just the right way.

This sorbet can be made with herbs such as tarragon or basil, or the seeds from half a vanilla bean, added to the sugar syrup, for an effective palate cleanser. And we love it with a few flakes of sea salt on top. Or, better yet, use it in a Salty Bitch (page 177) in a glass with a pink sea salt rim.

PREP With a peeler, remove 3 strips of zest from 1 grapefruit. Cut all of the grapefruits in half and squeeze 3 cups juice from them.

COOK Combine the grapefruit juice, zest, lemon juice, corn syrup, and sugar in a 4-quart saucepan and bring to a boil, stirring to dissolve the sugar. Transfer to a medium bowl, add the aromatics, if using, and let cool.

CHILL Remove the grapefruit zest. Place the sorbet base in the refrigerator and chill for at least 2 hours.

FREEZE Remove the sorbet base from the refrigerator and strain out any aromatics. Add the vodka. Remove the frozen canister from the freezer, assemble your ice cream machine, and turn it on. Pour the sorbet base into the canister and spin just until it is the consistency of very softly whipped cream.

   Pack the sorbet into a storage container. Press a sheet of parchment directly against the surface and seal with an airtight lid. Freeze in the coldest part of your freezer until firm, at least 4 hours.

Makes about 1 quart

4 grapefruits

3 tablespoons fresh lemon juice

½ cup light corn syrup

⅔ cup sugar

Optional aromatics: A few sprigs of tarragon, basil, or lavender; or ½ half vanilla bean split, seeds removed

¼ cup vodka

Grapefruit & Beet Shrub Sorbet
Substitute 1 tablespoon chardonnay vinegar and 2 tablespoons fresh beet juice for the lemon juice.

MELON JONESY SORBET

Sweet ripe cantaloupe and a lovely tawny port.

Jonesy is a fantastic tawny port that always gets crazy-high ratings, yet it retails for less than $20 a bottle. It has all the notes you want in tawny port: dried fruit, hazelnuts, and maple. This recipe is for a lovely late-summer sorbet and would be a stylish finish to a late lunch outdoors, or for a quiet moment out back in a rocking chair.

PREP Puree the cantaloupe in a food processor until smooth. Reserve 3 cups of the puree for the sorbet.

COOK Combine the corn syrup and sugar in a 4-quart saucepan and bring to a boil over medium heat, stirring until the sugar dissolves. Stir in the puree and port. Transfer to a medium bowl and let cool.

CHILL Place the sorbet base in the refrigerator and chill for at least 2 hours.

FREEZE Remove the frozen canister from the freezer, assemble your ice cream machine, and turn it on. Pour the sorbet base into the canister and spin just until it is the consistency of very softly whipped cream.
    Pack the sorbet into a storage container. Press a sheet of parchment directly against the surface and seal with an airtight lid. Freeze in the coldest part of your freezer until firm, at least 4 hours.

Makes about 1 quart

½ cantaloupe, peeled, seeded, and cut into small chunks

⅓ cup light corn syrup

⅓ cup sugar

1 cup Jonesy old tawny port (see Sources, page 200) or other high-quality tawny port

PLUM SAKE SORBET

Deep purple plums and plum-infused sake.
Sprightly, ultralight, refreshing, and fragrant.

Edna St. Vincent Millay's poem "The Plum Gatherer,"
along with her extended stay in Japan in the 1920s, inspired
this lovely warm-weather sorbet. I love Edna St. Vincent
Millay's poems. She was a modern person in the 1910s, a
time when modern thinking was rare for men or women.
One of my favorite lines from her is, "Who cares what
tripped a fallen woman?"

See page 161 for this sorbet's use in a parfait.

PREP Puree the plums in a food processor until smooth. Transfer to
a medium bowl.

COOK Combine the sugar and corn syrup in a 4-quart saucepan
and bring to a boil, stirring to dissolve the sugar. Whisk the hot sugar
syrup into the pureed plums.

CHILL Place the plum mixture in the refrigerator and chill for at
least 2 hours.

Strain the plum mixture through a sieve set over a bowl, then
add the sake and lemon juice.

FREEZE Remove the frozen canister from the freezer, assemble
your ice cream machine, and turn it on. Pour the sorbet base into
the canister and spin just until it is the consistency of very softly
whipped cream.

Pack the sorbet into a storage container. Press a sheet of
parchment directly against the surface and seal with an airtight lid.
Freeze in the coldest part of your freezer until firm, at least 4 hours.

Makes about 1 quart

2 pounds ripe black plums
(approximately 7), pitted
but unpeeled

⅔ cup sugar

½ cup light corn syrup

1 cup plum sake
(see Sources, page 200)

2 tablespoons fresh lemon juice

RED RASPBERRY SORBET

A sorbet that packs more flavor per spoonful than any other.
Makes striking cocktails.

Raspberry Sorbet is easy to find, and many cookbooks have recipes for it. I include it in this book for two reasons. First, raspberries are an example of a perfect fruit, like really great peaches (harder to find than raspberries), black currants, and ripe apricots. Sometimes you just want to respect that and leave well enough alone. Will tarragon or spices or mix-ins make the sorbet better? No. They may make it interesting, but nothing can make fresh raspberries more delightful.

Second, while you can't make a raspberry taste better, raspberries have a wonderful way of making other things taste better. Whether you use this sorbet in the center of the Macaroon Cake (page 96), serve it next to A Wiseman's Chocolate Cake (page 98), make a cocktail out of it (see page 178), or layer it into a "rainbow situation" (see Rainbow Frozen Yogurt, page 82), you can always depend on raspberries to give your dessert (or cocktail) a fresh, bright kick in the pants.

There is no water in this recipe, which is exactly how we make it at Jeni's—undiluted. The vodka makes it slightly less sweet because it allows us to reduce the sugar. It's the best raspberry sorbet I've ever tasted.

Makes about 1 quart

5 pints raspberries

1⅓ cups sugar

1 cup corn syrup

½ cup vodka

PREP Puree the raspberries in a food processor until smooth. Press through a sieve to remove the seeds.

COOK Combine the raspberry puree, sugar, and corn syrup in a 4-quart saucepan and bring to a boil over medium-high heat, stirring to dissolve the sugar. Remove from the heat, transfer to a medium bowl, and let cool.

CHILL Place the sorbet base in the refrigerator and chill for at least 2 hours.

FREEZE Remove the sorbet base from the refrigerator and add the vodka. Remove the frozen canister from the freezer, assemble your ice cream machine, and turn it on. Pour the sorbet base into the canister and spin just until it is the consistency of very softly whipped cream.

Pack the sorbet into a storage container. Press a sheet of parchment directly against the surface, and seal with an airtight lid. Freeze in the coldest part of your freezer until firm, at least 4 hours.

STONE FRUIT SORBET

Spirited stone fruits, of any variety, frozen into sorbet.

This sorbet can be made with whatever fruits look good in the market. Use a combination of fruits or just one type to make, for example, a nectarine and vodka sorbet. Or make one with black cherries and gin, or use whatever spirit and stone fruit you wish.

This sorbet is wonderful in the Lady of the Lake cocktail (page 179) or beside the Meringue Cake (page 102).

PREP Puree the fruit in a food processor until smooth.

COOK Combine the pureed fruit, sugar, and corn syrup in a 4-quart saucepan and bring to a simmer, stirring to dissolve the sugar. Remove from the heat, transfer to a medium bowl, and let cool.

CHILL Strain the mixture through a sieve into another bowl. Place in the refrigerator and chill for at least 2 hours.

FREEZE Remove the sorbet base from the refrigerator and stir in the vodka. Remove the frozen canister from the freezer, assemble your ice cream machine, and turn it on. Pour the sorbet base into the canister and spin just until it is the consistency of very softly whipped cream.

Pack the sorbet into a storage container. Press a sheet of parchment directly against the surface and seal with an airtight lid. Freeze in the coldest part of your freezer until firm, at least 4 hours.

Makes about 1 quart

2 pounds stone fruits (such as 1 medium peach peeled, 2 large plums, 4 apricots, and 16 dark red cherries), pitted

⅔ cup sugar

⅓ cup light corn syrup

¼ cup stone fruit vodka, preferably Middle West Spirits Stone Fruit Vodka (see Sources, page 200), or any vodka of your choice

WHEATGRASS, PEAR, & VINHO VERDE SORBET

*Crisp and green in flavor, with a delightful fuzziness—
like a shag carpet in color and texture.*

This sorbet is a nod to Walt Whitman—admittedly, a casual nod to his *Leaves of Grass*. Not literary but literal, as it is literally made with grass—and that is its singular connection.

Vinho verde is a light, effervescent white wine. Wheatgrass makes the sorbet greener, in color and flavor—it's very fresh tasting. And how can you resist the color and texture! Serve this between courses as a palate refresher or use it in a cocktail like the Sword in the Stone (page 177).

PREP Puree the pears and apples in a food processor until smooth. Combine the puree, wheatgrass juice, and vinho verde in a medium bowl.

COOK Combine the corn syrup, sugar, lemon juice, and turmeric, if using, in a medium saucepan, and bring to a boil, stirring to dissolve the sugar. Remove from the heat and stir into the pear and apple puree until thoroughly combined. Transfer to a medium bowl and let cool.

CHILL Place the sorbet base in the refrigerator and chill for at least 2 hours.

FREEZE Remove the frozen canister from the freezer, assemble your ice cream machine, and turn it on. Pour the sorbet base into the canister and spin just until it is the consistency of very softly whipped cream.

Pack the sorbet into a storage container. Press a sheet of parchment directly against the surface and seal with an airtight lid. Freeze in the coldest part of your freezer until firm, at least 4 hours.

Makes about 1 quart

2 ripe pears, halved, cored, and diced

2 Granny Smith apples, peeled, halved, cored, and diced

½ cup wheatgrass juice

½ cup vinho verde

¼ cup light corn syrup

1 cup sugar

1 tablespoon fresh lemon juice

¼ teaspoon turmeric (for color; optional)

In our bustling bakery, we make ingredients like marshmallows, gravel, and cookies for our ice creams and I create easy-to-assemble, ice-cream-centric dessert menus for chefs. In addition, I serve countless messy plates of ice cream with crisps, Bettes, cakes, pies, or tarts made with fruits of the season at work and at home. For all of them I rely on the amazing recipes in this chapter.

Almost every recipe here can be put to use in a multitude of ways. Consider the many personalities of Lady Cake (page 100). It is easy to make, incredibly simple in form (it's a 9-inch round pale yellow cake), and will become a go-to in your kitchen. The cake itself is the most moist, delicious cake I've ever eaten, and I think you will agree. This versatile cake is great by itself, but if you add ice cream you take it to an entirely different place. You can build an impressive Ice Cream Layer Cake (see pages 170–75) by fitting alternate layers of cake and ice cream into a mold and topping it with whipped cream and garnishes. This system can be altered in hundreds of ways to suit your needs, and the technique is truly painless. You might make Lady Cake often, but you will never make the same one twice.

Another versatile recipe is A Wiseman's Chocolate Cake (page 98), which is so chocolatey and velvety that you might think you're eating a truffle!

A riff on classic Southern-fried hand pies, Sweet Empanadas (page 140) can be assembled ahead and fried à la minute to be served hot with melting ice cream. Master the art of its very simple crust—mixing it, rolling it, and crimping the pies—and you are set to make any flavor you can think of. Directions for classic fruit empanadas are included, as well as other secret options found nowhere but in these pages. By making the Chocolate Glaze (page 189) extra thick, you can make a chocolate empanada that is like a gooey, bloated chocolate chip cookie—only with a lot more hot molten chocolate (and oohs and aahs from your guests). You can also stuff the empanadas with Corn Syrup Custard (page 183), which is like the inside of a pecan pie and absolutely amazing with ice cream. Please do make that.

The Sheet Pie (page 108), the Bettes (page 116), and the Cobblers (page 118) are all exactly what you came here for. I have made Bauer House Biscuits (page 122) hundreds of times with the same perfect results; you will use them for ice cream and berries, but keep them in mind for Southern-style ham salad, too. Peoria Corn Fritters (page 136) are also excellent with ice cream, but go ahead and make them for dinner, too—when served with a platter of fried chicken, they are a classic Midwestern staple.

Each dessert in this chapter is designed to be served with ice cream, but you will find that they are all delicious on their own. These are recipes that are foolproof, that are wonderful, that we never tire of in our kitchen. And, speaking of our little beloved test kitchen, it contains no professional equipment (quite the contrary), which means we are sure that you will be able to precisely replicate everything here in your own home. I've been disappointed in more cookbooks than I can count on that front, so it's important to me that these recipes are easily attainable. And they most deliciously are.

MACAROON CAKE

A sweet, nutty, orange-scented flourless cake made with almond, pistachio, or hazelnut flour.

This cake has a wonderful, delicate lightness but a very satisfying soft, candied texture that reminds me of the classic gooey butter cake made famous in St. Louis. As it bakes, a thin caramelized crust forms on top. The cake is sugary and fragrant, and it begs for ice cream and some slices of fruit or a drizzle of Hot Honey (page 188). It can be made with almond, pistachio, or hazelnut flour (finely ground nuts); almond is my favorite. I like the scent of orange zest with any of the nuts, but you can use any citrus zest.

Makes 8 to 10 servings

1¾ cups blanched whole almonds, 1¾ cups pistachios, or 2½ cups hazelnuts (about 14 ounces nuts)

6 large eggs, separated, at room temperature

1¼ cups sugar

Grated zest of 2 oranges

4 drops almond extract

Powdered sugar for dusting

Preheat the oven to 350°F. Butter the bottom of a 9-inch round cake pan and line with a round of parchment. Butter the parchment. Dust the pan with flour (using gluten-free flour if that is a concern) and shake out the excess.

Finely grind the almonds in a food processor until they are the consistency of coarse flour.

With an electric mixer, beat the egg yolks and sugar in a large bowl at high speed until pale and thick. Add the zest and almond extract, followed by the ground almonds, mixing very well.

Use clean beaters to beat the egg whites in a large bowl until stiff peaks form. Fold them into the yolk and almond mixture until well combined, being careful not to deflate the batter.

Pour the batter into the prepared pan. Bake for 40 minutes, or until the cake feels firm to the touch. Remove the cake from the oven and let it cool completely in the pan on a rack.

Invert the cake, remove the parchment, and turn right side up. Dust the top of the cake with confectioners' sugar just before serving.

ⓖ A WISEMAN'S CHOCOLATE CAKE

A rich, dark chocolate cake that melts in your mouth.

Pete Wiseman runs our busy bakery. He oversees all of the cakes, gravels, crusts, cookies, and anything else that comes out of our bakery kitchen and goes into our ice creams. He's also a talented cake baker. So when I couldn't get my chocolate cake to taste chocolatey enough, I turned to him.

This is what resulted from that consultation: his mom's recipe for the birthday cake that she made for Pete every year when he was growing up. And it could not be more wonderful. The cake is dense, but it melts in your mouth, and it soaks up ice cream like a dream. Oh, and it doesn't even require a mixer. It is as simple and delicious as can be. Thanks, Mrs. Wiseman! And happy birthday, Pete!

Position a rack in the middle of the oven and preheat the oven to 325°F. Butter a 9-inch round cake pan. Place a round of parchment in the bottom and butter it, then dust the pan with flour, and shake out the excess.

Whisk the flour, sugar, baking soda, and salt together in a large bowl.

Combine the chocolate and cocoa. Pour the hot coffee over the mixture and whisk until smooth. Whisk in the sour cream, egg, and vanilla. Stir the sour cream mixture into the flour mixture until just combined.

Scrape the batter into the cake pan and smooth the top with the back of a spoon. Bake for 40 to 45 minutes, until a toothpick inserted into the center comes out with just a few moist crumbs clinging to it. Let cool completely in the pan on a rack.

Invert the cake and remove the parchment. A dusting of powdered sugar is all this cake needs. Or try it topped with a layer of Chocolate Glaze, dusted with cocoa powder, and served with a scoop of ice cream as in the photo.

Makes 8 to 10 servings

1¼ cups unbleached all-purpose flour or gluten-free flour

1¼ cups sugar

½ teaspoon baking soda

½ teaspoon fine sea salt

4½ ounces unsweetened chocolate (99% cacao), finely chopped

¼ cup unsweetened cocoa powder

1 cup hot coffee

⅔ cup sour cream

1 large egg, beaten

2 teaspoons vanilla extract

Chocolate Glaze (page 189) for serving

Cocoa powder for dusting

Ice cream of your choice for serving

ⓖ LADY CAKE

An absolutely perfect yellow cake. Ready for a scoop of ice cream.

This rich, buttery cake needs nothing more than a dusting of powdered sugar, with perhaps a pile of fresh fruit on the side. Or top with some White Chocolate Glaze (page 189). Or split and fill it with ½ cup Blackberry Jam or one of the other jams (pages 182–83). And, of course, it goes well with a scoop of ice cream.

You can use regular cake flour, Bob's Red Mill wheat pastry flour (see Sources, page 200), cornstarch, or gluten-free flour. The wheat flour is a little earthier, with a little more tooth. Cornstarch produces a killer fine texture, with tiny little holes in the crumb and a caramelized flakiness on top.

Preheat the oven to 325°F. Butter the bottom of a 9-inch round cake pan. Line with a round of parchment and butter the paper. Dust with flour and shake out the excess.

Sift together the flour, baking soda, baking powder, and salt twice. Set aside. Combine the butter and sugar in a medium bowl and beat on high speed with an electric mixer until thick and pale, about 4 minutes, scraping down the sides of the bowl as needed. Add 1 egg and beat until thoroughly incorporated. Add the second egg and the vanilla and beat until thoroughly incorporated. Scrape down the sides of the bowl and beat the batter until smooth.

Add about one-third of the flour mixture and fold in gently with a rubber spatula. Fold in about half of the sour cream. Add another one-third of the flour mixture and fold it in, then fold in the remaining sour cream, and finally fold in the rest of the flour. Do not overmix.

Pour the batter into the prepared pan. Bake for 40 to 50 minutes, until a toothpick inserted into the center comes out with a few moist crumbs clinging to it. Cool in the pan on a rack for 10 minutes, then invert the cake onto a rack, remove the parchment, and let cool completely.

Makes 8 to 12 servings

1 cup cake flour (not self-rising), wheat pastry flour, cornstarch, or gluten-free flour

¼ teaspoon baking soda

½ teaspoon baking powder

¾ teaspoon fine sea salt

6 tablespoons (¾ stick) unsalted butter, softened

¾ cup sugar

2 large eggs, at room temperature

1 teaspoon vanilla extract

¾ cup sour cream or buttermilk

Beet Lady Cake

Mix 1 cup ground red beets with the sour cream and fold it into the flour mixture.

Zucchini Lady Cake

Shred 1 medium zucchini on a grater (about 1 cup). Squeeze the zucchini through cheesecloth until most of the water is gone. Meanwhile, proceed as directed, adding ¼ teaspoon ground cinnamon to the flour mixture. Mix the zucchini with the sour cream before folding it into the flour mixture.

ⓖ MERINGUE CAKE

The crisp shells burst into sugary air on contact.
Ethereal when stuffed with ice cream and served in slices.

What I love about this dessert is that it is absolutely minimalist—beautiful in its striking simplicity. Serve it on a clear glass plate, no garnish. But, of course, it also takes to being accompanied: fruit, sauce, flowers, or herbs are all right with this cake. Switch the ice cream inside depending on the occasion.

The cake is a breeze to make and assemble, but it will be at least a day and a half before you can eat it. In a way that's nice, because it means you can spread out the tasks. The meringues have to bake for 90 minutes, which gives you more than enough time to prep the ice cream base and chill it overnight. Then churn the ice cream right before you layer it between the disks—you'll want it soft, just out of the ice cream machine. Then put the cake in the freezer to harden for two or three hours.

Position the racks in the upper and lower thirds of the oven and preheat the oven to 200°F. Draw an 8-inch circle on each of two sheets of parchment, flip the paper over, and line two large baking sheets with the parchment.

Using an electric mixer, beat the egg whites in a large bowl at medium-low speed until just frothy, about 45 seconds. Add the cream of tartar, increase the speed to medium-high, and beat the egg whites until they are white and thick (the consistency of shaving cream), about 2 minutes. Slowly sprinkle in the sugar, beating until incorporated, then beat the whites until they form stiff peaks. (Turn the beater upside down: if the peaks do not droop, they are ready.)

Fit a pastry bag with a ¼-inch plain tip and fill with the meringue. Pipe the meringue in a spiral, in each traced circle, starting from the center and working your way out. Bake for 1½ hours, or until the exteriors of the meringues are smooth, dry, and firm. Turn off the oven and allow the meringues to cool in the oven for several hours.

Makes 8 servings

4 large egg whites, at room temperature

¼ teaspoon cream of tartar

1 cup sugar

Base for 1 batch ice cream of your choice (prepped the day before and chilled overnight)

Layer a piece of parchment between the meringues, wrap in plastic wrap, and freeze overnight.

The next day, remove the frozen canister from the freezer, assemble your ice cream machine, and turn it on. Pour the ice cream base into the freezer and spin until thick and creamy. When the ice cream is done, turn off the machine and leave the ice cream in it.

Remove one meringue shell from the freezer and place it upside down on a baking sheet lined with parchment. Working quickly, spoon and spread about 2 inches of ice cream onto the meringue, going to about ½ inch from the edge. Remove the second meringue from the freezer and quickly place it on top, right side up. Put the meringue cake back in the freezer and freeze for at least 4 hours, or up to 1 day.

Pack the remaining ice cream into a storage container. Press a sheet of parchment directly against the surface and seal with an airtight lid. Freeze in the coldest part of your freezer until firm, at least 4 hours, to serve at another time.

To serve, remove the cake from the freezer, slice into 8 pieces, and serve immediately.

Ⓖ MOCHI CAKE

A buttery, not-too-sweet rice flour cake has a delightful chewiness.

This is one of our favorite recipes. We originally made it to cut into cubes and throw into our bubble-gum-pink Magnolia Mochi Ice Cream (page 45). It has an enjoyably chewy texture when frozen and is soft, buttery, and dense at room temperature.

If you so desire, you can trim off the outer layer to give the cake super-sharp square corners. Aesthetically, that's pretty cool, and you can't do that with other cakes. You can then slice it into crisp-edged squares or rectangles or cubes of whatever size. Sauté them in butter until golden and crispy on the outside, and *wow!* Or brush them with butter and put them on the grill. Serve these with tea-infused or flower-scented ice cream and with exotic fruits, like fresh rambutans on the half-shell.

Makes 8 to 10 servings

2 cups sweet rice flour

1¼ cups sugar

1¾ teaspoons baking powder

Pinch of ground cinnamon

1⅓ cups evaporated milk

1¼ cups unsweetened coconut milk

2 large eggs, at room temperature

1½ teaspoons vanilla extract

5½ tablespoons unsalted butter, melted

Position a rack in the center of the oven and preheat the oven to 350°F. Butter a 9-by-5-inch loaf pan.

Sift together the rice flour, sugar, baking powder, and cinnamon into a large bowl.

Add the evaporated milk, coconut milk, eggs, vanilla, and butter in a bowl, and whisk to combine. Create a small well in the middle of the dry ingredients, pour in the liquid ingredients, and stir until fully combined.

Pour the batter into the loaf pan and bake for 35 minutes.

Rotate the cake pan and bake for about 35 minutes longer, until a toothpick inserted into the center of the cake comes out with a few moist crumbs clinging to it. Cool the cake in the pan on a rack for 10 minutes, then invert onto a rack to cool completely.

Mochi Cake Croutons

Cut the mochi into 1-inch cubes. Melt 1 tablespoon unsalted butter in a large sauté pan. Add the cubes, let sit until golden on the bottom, and then repeat on each side. Serve scattered around ice cream and fruit.

Grilled Mochi Cake Slices

Preheat a grill to medium-high. Cut the mochi into ½-inch-thick slices. Brush with melted butter and set on the grill. Turn when grill marks appear, 2 to 3 minutes, and grill until marked on the second side. Serve with ice cream and fruit.

STONE-GROUND-GRITS PUDDING CAKE

A cake with a soft pudding-like texture and the flavors of corn and honey.

My great-grandfather Floyd Britton, great midwesterner that he was, used to live in a cabin on a lake in Wisconsin not far from Chicago. We'd vacation there and spend our days jumping off the dock into the freezing lake, fishing, and tooling around in his pontoon boat. Floyd's signature dish, which I recall him making daily, was mush—cornmeal mixed with water and a little salt, boiled vigorously, cooled, and solidified in a shallow pan, then sliced and grilled or panfried in butter. My great-grandfather would serve it with fresh tomatoes or maple syrup (from his trees), bacon, and eggs, a great feast of a meal. I love it now, but I hated it then. Maybe it was just the name.

He would have called this "Mush Cake." If you are a fan of rice or tapioca pudding, or bread pudding, you will love it as I do. It's essentially a pudding when it's hot and a sliceable pudding cake when cooled. We cut cubes of the room-temperature pudding cake and serve them with our Buttermilk Soft-Serve (page 68) or Honeyed Buttermilk Ice Cream (page 48). If you would like to do this, you can make the cake up to three days ahead, wrap it in plastic, and store it in the refrigerator.

Makes 8 to 10 servings

3 cups lukewarm water

¾ cup stone-ground grits

1¼ cups unbleached all-purpose flour or gluten-free flour

1½ teaspoons baking powder

½ teaspoon fine sea salt

½ pound (2 sticks) unsalted butter, softened

1 cup plus 2 tablespoons sugar

4 large eggs, at room temperature

½ cup sour cream or buttermilk

Ancho-Orange Caramel Sauce (page 187) for serving

Ice cream of your choice for serving

Bring the water to a boil in a 2-quart saucepan. Add the grits, whisking constantly, then cook, stirring occasionally, until they are tender and pull away slightly from the sides of the pan, 25 to 30 minutes. Remove from the heat and let cool to room temperature.

Position a rack in the center of the oven and preheat the oven to 350°F. Butter a 9-by-13-inch baking dish.

Whisk the flour, baking powder, and salt together in a medium bowl.

Using an electric mixer, beat the butter and sugar in a large bowl until light and fluffy, about 2 minutes. Add the eggs one at a time, beating well after each addition. Beat in the sour cream and grits, then add the flour mixture and beat just until incorporated. Spread the batter evenly in the prepared pan.

Bake the cake for 35 to 40 minutes, until it is golden and a toothpick inserted into the center comes out with a few moist crumbs clinging to it. Transfer the cake to a rack and cool in the pan for 5 minutes, then run a knife around the edges of the cake to loosen it, invert it onto a rack, and let cool completely.

Serve with a healthy dose of Ancho-Orange Caramel Sauce and a scoop or two of ice cream.

SHEET PIE

A buttery crust + a thin layer of fresh fruit = a large flat pie.

Sheet Pie (or slab pie) is a shallow double-crust pie, usually with a fruit filling. Because there is less filling than in a traditional pie, a good crust becomes all the more important. It's baked in a quarter sheet pan, which can be found in kitchen supply stores and online. Sheet pies are easier to serve than regular pies: there's no awkward shoveling out of the first piece and no fruit oozing out everywhere.

For the crust, I am in the half-butter, half-shortening camp. Shortening gives the crust more flakiness and butter gives it flavor. I use all-natural shortening rather than the hydrogenated kind.

Makes 8 to 10 servings

DOUGH

3¾ cups unbleached all-purpose flour

1½ teaspoons fine sea salt

¾ cup cold vegetable shortening

12 tablespoons (1½ sticks) unsalted butter, cut into bits and chilled, or vegetable shortening

½ cup plus 1 tablespoon ice water

1 large egg

1 teaspoon water

FRUIT FILLING

3 pounds apples, plums, peaches, or cherries, sliced, peeled, and cored; or rhubarb, sliced into ½-inch pieces; or whole blackberries, raspberries, or blueberries

½ teaspoon ground cinnamon, cardamom, or nutmeg

1 tablespoon fresh lemon juice

½ cup sugar

¼ cup all-purpose flour

To make the dough, blend the flour and salt in a large bowl. Using two knives or a pastry cutter, cut in the shortening and butter until the mixture resembles coarse meal. Stir in the ice water and blend well.

Form the dough into a ball and knead it lightly with the heel of your hand on a work surface for a few seconds to distribute the fats evenly. Divide the dough in half. Shape each half into a ball, flatten into a disk, and wrap in plastic wrap. Refrigerate for at least 1 hour.

Meanwhile, to make the filling, put the fruit in a large bowl, add all of the remaining ingredients, and stir until the fruit is evenly coated.

Preheat the oven to 350°F.

When the dough has rested for an hour, lightly flour a work surface and roll out one piece of dough into a 12-by-16-inch rectangle. Roll the dough up on the rolling pin and transfer it to a quarter sheet pan, centering it in the pan and pressing the dough up against the edges.

Pour the filling into the pan and spread it into a thin layer.

Roll out the second piece of dough to the size of your quarter sheet pan. Cut a few holes in it with a cookie cutter, so the steam will be able to escape, or pierce the dough several times with a fork. Place it over the filling. Fold the edges of the bottom crust over the top crust. Beat the egg with the 1 teaspoon water to make an egg wash, and brush it over the top of the crust.

Bake for 45 minutes, or until evenly browned and the edges have turned extra-golden.

Serve immediately, or let cool on a rack and serve warm or at room temperature.

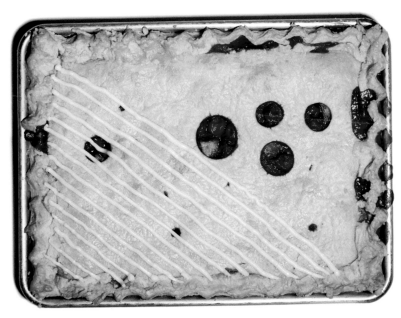

FRENCH ICE CREAM TARTS

Classic, gorgeous, striking, and delish.

In the French bakery where I worked years ago, we made hundreds of these tarts every day. Theirs were filled with a delicious pastry cream, made with equal parts of fresh whipped cream and chilled freshly made egg yolk custard, and topped with glazed fruits of all varieties. I was in charge of cranking out the tart shells for these beauties. It was a delicious job and I loved every moment.

This is the ice cream version of those tarts. I like to fill them with our Salty Vanilla Frozen Custard, because it tastes so close to the pastry cream we made daily in the bakery. Make the shells in advance using Sugar Dough and get them into the freezer. Then, bring out a few at a time, fill them about two-thirds of the way full with softened ice cream, and return them to the freezer until hardened.

Right before you serve them, melt some store-bought or homemade apricot jam over very low heat and toss handfuls of berries, sliced plums, peaches, or nectarines into just enough jam to made them shine. Whip some cream if you want. Then remove the shells from the freezer and pile as much fruit on top as will fit, or arrange it in patterns. Top the tarts with whipped cream and take them to the table. Don't put them back in the freezer, because the fruit will freeze and sink into the ice cream.

Makes 12 tarts

1 batch Sugar Dough (recipe follows)

About 1 quart ice cream of your choice, such as Salty Vanilla Frozen Custard (page 60)

½ cup apricot jam, storebought or homemade

3 pints fresh fruit of your choice, chilled

Whipped Cream (page 191; optional)

Preheat the oven to 350°F. Cut out 12 parchment circles and line twelve 4-inch tart pans.

Roll out the dough about ⅛ inch thick. Cut out twelve 5-inch rounds. Ease each round into a tart pan. Place on a cookie sheet.

Bake for 20 minutes, until golden. Allow to cool completely on a rack, remove the tart shells from the tins, and freeze for at least 30 minutes.

Remove the tart shells from the freezer, fill halfway with freshly made or softened ice cream, and return to the freezer for at least 1 hour. Toss the chilled fruit with the apricot jam. Remove the tart shells from the freezer and top with piles or patterns of glazed fruit and whipped cream. Serve.

SUGAR DOUGH

A traditional sweet dough for tarts.

I made pâte sucrée every day when I worked in a French bakery. I cut rounds of it and coaxed them gently into tart shells, and I used it to make linzer cookies by the hundreds. The dough is sweet but not too sweet. It's very buttery, more cookie-like than piecrust-like.

I add some cream cheese and heavy cream to the recipe, which make it a little flakier. Cream cheese is not light, but the result is lighter than the traditional all-butter dough.

Put the flour, sugar, butter, and cream cheese into a food processor and pulse until the mixture looks like almond meal. (You can also rub the butter and cream cheese into the flour and sugar with your hands. Work quickly so the butter doesn't melt.) Add the egg yolks and cream and pulse (or continue mixing with your hands until evenly blended).

Divide the dough in half. Knead half the dough until it comes together in a ball, then press it into a flat disk about 2 inches thick. Do the same with the second half. Wrap each portion of dough in plastic wrap and chill for at least 1 hour before using.

Makes enough for 12 hand tarts or Piekies

1½ cups unbleached all-purpose flour

⅓ cup sugar

8 tablespoons (1 stick) unsalted butter, cut into ½-inch cubes and chilled

2 ounces (4 tablespoons) cream cheese

2 large egg yolks, lightly beaten

2 tablespoons very cold heavy cream

MAKING THE TART SHELLS

This dough is super-easy to make and fun to work with. The shells can be filled with many different things and frozen for up to three months.

THE STEPS

Pulse the ingredients in a food processor. Remove from the bowl, divide in half, knead into a ball, flatten it with the back of your hand, wrap in plastic wrap, and chill for 1 hour. Repeat with the second half.

Throw a little flour on the work surface to prevent sticking.

Remove one disk of dough from the fridge and roll out to ⅛ inch thick.

Cut with a 5-inch round cookie cutter.

Ease each piece of dough into a parchment-lined 4-inch tart pan.

Gently pat the dough up against the sides and bake (see page 111).

PIEKIES

Sugar dough rounds with slices of fruit and sugar baked as small open-faced pies.

What's better with ice cream than pie? Here is a pie in cookie form. Piekies are made minimally, with just slices of fruit or a couple of berries. Then they can be used to garnish a bowl of ice cream. You can make a batch using many different fruits and set out a whole platter or cookie stand of Piekies as a colorful adornment to your dessert table. Or put them out with some ice cream in containers on the table and let your guests serve themselves.

Makes 12 to 24 Piekies

Sugar Dough (page 112)

1 cup sugar

1 tablespoon cornstarch

1 pound strawberries, plums, peaches, nectarines, and/or apples, peeled, pitted, and sliced very thin using a mandoline or very sharp knife, or cherries, pitted and diced, or a combination

Preheat the oven to 350°F. Butter two baking sheets or line them with parchment paper.

Roll out the dough about ⅛ inch thick. Using a biscuit or cookie cutter, cut into 2½- to 3-inch circles and place on the baking sheets.

Blend the sugar and cornstarch in a small bowl. Generously coat each slice of fruit by dipping it into the sugar mixture, turning to coat. Lay one slice in the center of a dough circle, then arrange additional fruit slices around it (the fruit will shrink while baking, so it's okay to have slices reach, or even extend beyond, the edges of the dough rounds). Overlap the fruit as needed. Repeat with all of the remaining dough and fruit.

Bake for 25 minutes, until golden. Remove from the oven and let cool on the pan for 2 minutes, then transfer to a wire rack and allow to cool completely. Serve immediately next to your favorite ice cream or keep refrigerated for up to 3 days.

APPLE RHUBARB BETTE

Fresh fruit topped casserole-style with buttery cubes of bread and baked.

I have no idea why Bettys are called Bettys, but my grandmother is Bette, so I spell it as she does.

This is one of those MacGyver recipes that you can pull together with ingredients you already have, or easily alter according to what's in season. The most decadent version is made with cubed croissants, which add butteriness and get really crisp on the top. It's also great with brioche or, frankly, any bread you have on hand, even the bagged stuff. The mainstay is 2 pounds of fruit. A good rule of thumb when it comes to the fruit is to use a blend of sweet and tart, so since a classic Bette is made with apples, I mix tart green ones with a sweeter variety. It punches up all the flavors. Feel free to use a different combination of spices, too, if you prefer.

Many other fruit combinations for Bettes are great—for example, Bartlett pears and blackberries; black plums and nectarines; and the variation I present, peaches and Bing cherries.

Makes 9 servings

1 pound Honeycrisp or Pink Lady apples, peeled, cored, and sliced

1 pound rhubarb, trimmed and cut into ¼ inch slices

¼ teaspoon ground cinnamon

⅛ teaspoon ground nutmeg

½ teaspoon fine sea salt

2 tablespoons fresh lemon juice

1 cup sugar

1 tablespoon unbleached all-purpose flour

10 ounces croissants or brioche (crusts removed), cut into 1-inch dice (about 4½ cups)

12 tablespoons (1½ sticks) unsalted butter, melted

Preheat the oven to 375°F. Butter an 8-by-8-inch baking dish.

Combine the apples and rhubarb in a medium bowl. Add the cinnamon, nutmeg, salt, lemon juice, ¾ cup of the sugar, and the flour, and toss until the sugar has dissolved and the sliced fruit is completely coated.

Combine the bread and the remaining ¼ cup sugar in another medium bowl. Pour ½ cup of the melted butter over the bread and toss gently, so that the cubes mostly remain intact, to coat.

To assemble the Bette, spread two-thirds of the fruit over the bottom of the baking dish. Scatter one-third of the bread over the fruit. Repeat with the remaining fruit and bread.

Pour the remaining ¼ cup butter over the top and cover with aluminum foil. Bake for 40 minutes. Remove the foil and continue baking for 10 to 15 minutes, until brown. Serve hot from the oven.

Bing Cherry & Peach Bette
Substitute 10 ounces fresh cherries, pitted and halved, or frozen cherries, halved, and 1 pound peaches, peeled, pitted, and sliced, for the apples and rhubarb.

BLUEBERRY COBBLER

Fresh fruit, very saucy, with Sweet Cream Shortcakes soaking it all up.

This cobbler has a generous amount of fruit (as do the variations), which releases a good deal of sauce during baking. The fruit is topped with Sweet Cream Shortcakes spooned into nine servings. Cobblers can be made with virtually any fruit, and served with any ice cream, giving you the chance to make the right dessert for your moment.

Makes 9 servings

2½ pounds blueberries

1 cup sugar

¼ teaspoon fine sea salt

Juice of 1 lemon

½ of dough for Sweet Cream Shortcakes (page 124)

Butter an 8-by-8-inch baking pan. Combine the blueberries with the sugar, salt, and lemon juice in a medium bowl, tossing to coat. Add to the prepared pan. Spoon the batter over the fruit, making 9 equal biscuits.

Preheat the oven to 375°F.

Bake the cobber for 35 minutes, until the tops of the biscuits are golden and the berries are bubbling. Remove from the oven and allow to cool slightly before serving.

Peach Cobbler
Substitute 2½ pounds peaches, peeled, pitted, and sliced, for the blueberries.

Peach, Cherry, & Blackberry Cobbler
Substitute 1 pound peaches, peeled, pitted, and sliced, 1 pound pitted cherries, and 8 ounces blackberries for the blueberries.

PEAR & BLACKBERRY CRISP WITH ALMOND STREUSEL

Fruit + streusel + ice cream = always in style.

Crisps are adaptable to whatever fruit you want to use or what is in season: apples, cherries, pears, peaches, or apricots, or a combination. Spice the fruit up a little, toss it all together, and top with this basic streusel, which you can give character to by adding almonds, coconut, etc. You can also spice the streusel up however you'd like with cinnamon, ginger, or cardamom, a lot or a little, a combination or a single spice note.

Crisps can be served straight from the baking dish, with a few pint containers of ice cream on the side. Or, for a stylish presentation, bake them in ½-pint Weck jars. Serve in the jars on cute plates, with a scoop of complementary ice cream, such as Graham Cracker Ice Cream (page 46), on top.

Crisps are a breeze to prepare, and it's easy to give this recipe its own unique character each time you make it, so it will always feel new and fresh—even though it could not be more traditional.

Makes 9 servings

STREUSEL
¾ cup unbleached all-purpose flour

¼ cup packed dark brown sugar

¼ teaspoon ground cinnamon

⅛ teaspoon ground nutmeg

5 tablespoons unsalted butter, diced and chilled

¾ cup sliced almonds, shaved unsweetened coconut flakes, or oats

FRUIT FILLING
1 pound Comice or Bartlett pears (about 2 pears), peeled, cored, and cut into ½-inch-thick wedges

2 cups blackberries

¾ cup sugar

2 tablespoons all-purpose flour

¼ teaspoon ground cinnamon

⅛ teaspoon grated nutmeg

½ teaspoon fine sea salt

2 tablespoons butter

Preheat the oven to 325°F.

To make the streusel, mix the flour, sugar, cinnamon, and nutmeg in a small bowl. Add the butter and rub it in with your fingertips until the mixture resembles coarse meal. Add the almonds, and rub the mixture with your fingertips until small clumps form. Spread on a baking sheet.

Bake the streusel for 20 minutes. Fluff with a fork and, if necessary, bake a few minutes longer, until golden brown. (Bake for an additional 20 minutes if using as an ice cream mix-in.) Remove from the oven and let cool. Increase the oven temperature to 375°F.

Butter an 8-by-8-inch baking dish. Toss the pears, berries, sugar, flour, spices, and salt together in a large bowl. Transfer to the prepared dish. Dot with the butter. Distribute the streusel evenly over the top.

Bake for about 45 minutes, until the fruit juices are bubbling and thickened and the streusel is deep brown. Cool slightly before serving.

BAUER HOUSE BISCUITS

Light and fluffy biscuits, perfect for ice cream sandwiches, or as Berry Biscuit Cakes, with berries and ice cream.

I call these Bauer House Biscuits because they fall somewhere between a biscuit and a Parker House roll. They are buttery and crispy on the outside and a dream inside. I think you're gonna love them.

Unlike the Sweet Cream Shortcakes (page 124) and biscuits in general, these are made with yeast. The yeast, as well as the butter, in the recipe makes the dough a joy to work with. The biscuits you'll turn out will be fluffier than most, and, yes, yeasty. Perfect for soaking up ice cream and berry juices, they are also good the next day.

I spent a year making croissants from scratch in a French bakery, so I use a similar folding-and-rolling technique to produce flaky layers in these biscuits. The yeast dough and the butter create pockets of air and rise. Light yet hearty, buttery, yet yeasty, these biscuits are perfection.

Although the biscuits are easy to make, they do require some time to rise. Allow the dough to sit overnight, or up to 3 days, in your refrigerator to develop a more complex yeasty flavor. Then cut them, let rise in a warm place until they almost double in size, and bake them.

Makes about 13 biscuits

¼ ounce (1 packet) active dry yeast

¼ cup lukewarm water (105° to 115°F)

2 tablespoons sugar

3¼ cups self-rising flour, preferably White Lily bleached

6 tablespoons (¾ stick) cold unsalted butter, cut into tablespoons

1 cup buttermilk, at room temperature

2 tablespoons salted butter, softened, for the tops of the biscuits

Combine the yeast, lukewarm water, and 1 teaspoon of the sugar in a medium bowl. Set aside until the yeast looks foamy, about 10 minutes.

Stir together the flour and the remaining 5 teaspoons sugar in a large bowl. Use a pastry cutter or two knives to cut in the butter until the mixture looks mealy. (Alternatively, combine the flour, sugar, and butter in a food processor and pulse about 20 times, until the mixture looks mealy.)

Stir the buttermilk into the dissolved yeast. Using a fork, stir in the flour mixture just until it is moistened and you have a shaggy dough. Cover and refrigerate overnight, or for up to 3 days.

Remove the dough from the refrigerator and knead it briefly, about 8 turns, until it comes together and the surface looks smooth. On a very lightly floured surface, roll it out into a 7-by-11-inch rectangle about ¾ inch thick, flouring the rolling pin sparingly as needed. Brush any excess flour off the dough and fold one short end over the center of the dough, then fold over the other end so that the dough is folded in thirds. Turn the dough one turn so that a short end is toward you and roll out to about ¾ inch thick. Brush off any excess flour and fold the dough into thirds again. Turn the dough once again and gently roll out to about ½ inch thick; the finished rectangle will be about 7 inches by 11 inches.

With a 2-inch round cutter, stamp out 13 biscuits. Be sure that the dough is still very cold (chill it if necessary), so that the cutter cuts cleanly; if the dough is too soft, the cutter can seal the sides and the biscuits won't rise. And be careful not to twist the cutter, or the biscuits will rise unevenly.

Arrange the biscuits in an ungreased 9-inch round cake pan, 10 around the outside and 3 in the middle. Gather the scraps together, roll out, and cut more biscuits. Put these in a smaller pan for a treat for you or your little ones—they won't look perfect, but they will still taste good. Cover the biscuits with a damp lint-free towel and let rise in a warm place (about 80°F) until they have doubled in volume, about 2 hours.

Note: The biscuits can also be cut into 2-inch squares and baked in a 9-by-9-inch pan.

Preheat the oven to 425°F.

Bake the biscuits until they are golden brown on top, about 13 minutes. Remove the biscuits from the oven, slather them with the softened butter, and let cool before serving.

Fried Biscuits

You can also fry these like donuts. What you retrieve from the hot oil after a few moments will be crisp on the outside and hot and yeasty on the inside—a cross between a biscuit and a donut, and a perfect companion to ice cream with honey or berries. Drop them into a bag of cinnamon sugar or powdered sugar while they are still hot. Use them for the sundae on page 155.

Cut out the biscuits and let rise as directed. Pour 3 inches of oil into a large deep pot (or use a deep-fryer) and heat the oil to 365°F. Fry the biscuits, turning once, until they are puffy and deep golden brown, 2 to 3 minutes per side. Remove the biscuits from the oil and drain them briefly on paper towels, then toss the biscuits with cinnamon sugar or powdered sugar.

SWEET CREAM SHORTCAKES

Easy-to-make shortcake with superior texture and wonderful buttery flavor.

The texture of this shortcake reminds me of the famous biscuits at the Loveless Cafe in Nashville, which is why we use this recipe to crumble into one of our most popular flavors ever: Cream Biscuits with Peach Jam Ice Cream (page 36). This cake is great to serve with generous spoonfuls of Hot Honey (page 188), Sweet Cream Ice Cream (page 28), and a few fresh blackberries—follow the instructions on the facing page. Of course, it will make a grand strawberry shortcake, too, because it excels at absorbing sauce. Composed of just three ingredients, it comes together in moments. I spread it into all four corners of a quarter sheet pan using my hands, then throw it in the oven. You can sprinkle it with sugar if you wish before baking, or just top it with melted butter when it comes out of the oven.

Makes 9 to 12 servings

3 cups self-rising flour, preferably White Lily

4 tablespoons cold unsalted butter

2⅔ cups heavy cream

Preheat the oven to 450°F. Butter a quarter sheet pan.

Put the flour and cold butter in a food processor and pulse 15 times. Add the cream and pulse until the dough comes together into a shaggy mess.

Turn the dough out onto a lightly floured surface and press it together. Fold the dough in half, then fold it over itself two or three times, just until it is no longer clumpy. Spread the dough onto the pan—it spreads easily, so you can use your hands.

Bake for 20 to 25 minutes, or until lightly golden brown. Remove the cake from the oven and cool on a rack.

Buckwheat Shortcakes
Use 2 cups self-rising flour (not 3) and 1 cup buckwheat flour.

Sweet Cream Shortcakes with Hot Honey, Sweet Cream Ice Cream, and Blackberries
After baking, make fork holes all over the dough in the pan. Pour 1 cup of warm Hot Honey (page 188) over the warm cake as evenly as possible. Let sit for 30 minutes to soak in fully. Cut the shortcake into 9 to 12 even squares and place each one on a plate. Top with a scoop of Sweet Cream Ice Cream (page 28) and another drizzle of Hot Honey. Add a few fresh blackberries and a dollop of Honey Whipped Cream (page 191).

JAKE'S CHOCOLATE TRUFFLE COOKIES

A very dark, rich, and dense chocolate truffle cookie.

We wanted a really dark cookie that would stay relatively soft when frozen into an ice cream sandwich. Not a cakey whoopee-pie cookie, but something like the cookie equivalent of a flourless chocolate cake. You know how most chocolate cookies don't taste very rich and dark? Chef Jake, who works in our test kitchen, solved that with this cookie. It's almost truffle-like, with lots of butter and just enough flour to hold it together.

Melt the butter and dark chocolate in a double boiler over low heat, stirring occasionally until completely melted. Cool completely.

Combine the flour, cocoa powder, salt, and baking soda in a small bowl. Set aside.

Using an electric mixer, beat the eggs and sugar in a large bowl on high speed until light and fluffy, about 2 minutes. Add the vanilla, then add the melted chocolate and butter and beat for 1 to 2 minutes, until combined.

Scrape down the sides of the bowl and, using a large rubber spatula, stir in the dry ingredients just until incorporated. Fold in the chocolate chips. Cover with plastic wrap and refrigerate for at least 4 hours.

Position a rack in the center of the oven and preheat the oven to 325°F. Line a baking sheet with parchment paper.

Wet your hands with water and roll the dough into 2-inch balls, placing them about 2 inches apart on the lined baking sheet. Work quickly, and if you are baking the cookies in batches, refrigerate the remaining dough between rounds.

Bake for 12 to 13 minutes, until the edges have risen slightly and the center is mostly set. Remove from the oven and let cool on the pan for at least 10 minutes, then transfer to a rack and let cool completely.

Makes about 16 cookies

- 8 tablespoons (1 stick) unsalted butter
- 8 ounces dark chocolate (64% cacao or higher), coarsely chopped
- ½ cup unbleached all-purpose flour or gluten-free flour
- 2 tablespoons Dutch-processed cocoa powder (99% cacao)
- ¼ teaspoon fine sea salt
- ¼ teaspoon baking soda
- 2 large eggs, at room temperature
- ½ cup sugar
- 2 teaspoons vanilla extract
- 1 cup dark chocolate chips (64% cacao or higher)

TO ASSEMBLE ICE CREAM SANDWICHES

Put the cookies on a sheet pan and freeze for 1 hour. Soften 1 quart of ice cream until scoopable. I like to keep it simple and use Sweet Cream Ice Cream (page 28), but you can use whatever flavor you want. Remove the cookies from the freezer and, working quickly, scoop 2 to 4 ounces of ice cream onto a cookie. Smoosh the ice cream by placing another cookie on top. Repeat. When you're finished assembling all the sandwiches, return them to the freezer for at least 2 hours to harden.

OATMEAL CREAM SANDWICHES

Soft, chewy oatmeal cookies, with ice cream inside.

We sell countless numbers of these ice cream sandwiches in our shops. The cookies stay soft when frozen, so you won't have to gnaw on them, and you can fill them with any ice cream you want to. The Frozen Skyr (page 80) and the Buttermilk Soft-Serve (page 68) are both fantastic options, as is Sweet Cream Ice Cream (page 28).

Rather than sandwiching them into a cream pie, you can also serve the oatmeal cookies on the side, accompanying your favorite flavors.

Position a rack in the center of the oven and preheat the oven to 325°F. Line two baking sheets with parchment.

Combine the flour, oats, baking soda, and cinnamon in a bowl and mix thoroughly. Using an electric mixer, beat the butter in a large bowl until smooth and creamy. Add the sugar and salt and beat until

Makes 24 cookies

1½ cups unbleached all-purpose flour

2 cups quick-cooking oats (instant oatmeal)

1 teaspoon baking soda

¼ teaspoon ground cinnamon

½ pound (2 sticks) unsalted butter, softened

1½ cups packed light brown sugar

¾ teaspoon fine sea salt

1 teaspoon vanilla extract

2 large eggs, at room temperature

1 quart Farmstead Cheese & Guava Jam Ice Cream (page 34), or other ice cream of your choice

the mixture is light in color and fluffy; scrape down the sides of the bowl as needed. Add the vanilla extract and beat just to combine. Add the eggs one at a time, beating well after each addition. The batter should be smooth and creamy.

Add half of the dry ingredients and mix on low speed until just combined. Add the remaining flour and mix until combined. Be careful not to overwork the dough.

Use a 1-ounce scoop to portion the dough onto the baking sheets, spacing the cookies about 2 inches apart. (If you don't have a scoop, use 2 tablespoons of dough to roll each cookie.) Slightly flatten the cookies with the heel of your hand or with the back of a wooden spoon. Bake the cookies for 7 minutes. Rotate the pan and bake for 4 to 6 more minutes, or until the cookies are very lightly browned on the edges but barely set in the center. Let the cookies cool for 10 minutes on the baking sheet. Then stack them in a container or in a 1-gallon Ziploc freezer bag and freeze for 2 hours.

To assemble the cream sandwiches, place 3 frozen cookies on a sheet pan. Put a rounded scoop (2 to 3 ounces) of slightly softened ice cream on each cookie. Top with three more cookies, squishing the two cookies together until the ice cream flattens out and meets the outer edges.

Place the fully assembled cream sandwiches back into the freezer and repeat with the remaining cookies.

CREAM PUFFS, ÉCLAIRS, OR RING CAKE

Toasty cream puff pastry filled with custard ice cream and topped with a sweet flavorful glaze or icing.

This recipe is inspired by the great big cream puffs that they serve at Schmidt's Sausage Haus in Columbus. Theirs are piled high with a salty vanilla custard cream and are the most amazing things you will ever put in your mouth. With ice cream and drippy chocolate glaze, they are classic, elegant showstoppers.

A great thing about the puff recipe is that you can make big ones or small ones, and if you make long thin ones, you have éclairs. If you lay out the whole batch on a pan in a ring, you can slice it in half and fill it with ice cream to make a ring cake. Either drizzle chocolate glaze over or dust with

1 cup lukewarm water

4 tablespoons (½ stick) unsalted butter, cut into pieces

1 cup unbleached all-purpose flour or gluten-free flour

4 large eggs, at room temperature

Salty Vanilla Frozen Custard (page 60) or Salty Goat's-Milk Chocolate Frozen Custard (page 60)

Chocolate Glaze (page 189; use 4 tablespoons whole milk)

powdered sugar. You can even plant nuts, toasted seeds, gravels, or candies in the chocolate glaze to decorate. They are truly easy to make and every bit as delicious as they look.

I keep the cooled puffs at room temperature and add the ice cream quickly right before I serve them. I don't freeze the whole thing because the puffs lose their lovely softness in the freezer.

My cousin Deb in San Diego, who inspired me to make this in a ring-cake form, uses gluten-free flour, and you won't notice the difference. A great gluten-free option.

Preheat the oven to 400°F.

Combine the water and butter in a medium heavy saucepan and bring to a boil, stirring to melt the butter. Pour in all the flour and mix until the mixture forms a ball. Remove from the heat and beat in the eggs one at a time with an electric mixer.

For Cream Puffs

Spoon six 4-inch individual mounds of dough onto an ungreased cookie sheet (for smaller puffs, make twelve 2-inch mounds). Bake until golden brown, about 45 minutes. Remove from the oven and let cool.

For Éclairs

Fit a pastry bag with a ¼-inch plain tip, then pipe six to twelve 4-inch strips onto an ungreased cookie sheet. Bake until golden brown, about 45 minutes. Remove from the oven and let cool.

For a Ring Cake

Drop even spoonfuls of dough onto an ungreased cookie sheet to make a 12-inch oval. Bake until golden brown, 45 to 50 minutes. Remove from the oven and let cool.

To Assemble

Prepare the glaze. Slice the cream puffs, éclairs, or ring cake in half. Fill with the ice cream, and put the top(s) back on.

For cream puffs, dip the top of each puff into the chocolate. For éclairs, generously spoon the glaze over them. For the ring cake, stir an additional 5 tablespoons of milk into the glaze; drizzle it over the ring cake.

To serve, arrange the pastries or slices of the cake on plates.

KATAIFI NESTS

Crispy shreds of phyllo brushed with honey butter, the perfect cushion for ice cream.

Kataifi nests fall somewhere between garnish, pastry, and entertainment. Kataifi is available in Middle Eastern or Greek groceries, and it can be mounded into shapes or formed into nests and baked. The kataifi is crispy, and when brushed with honey butter, it becomes sweet; I also sprinkle on a few flakes of sea salt.

I fell in love with kataifi in 1997, when I spent most of the summer on a small island in Greece called Ikaria. In an all-night café in the town of Therma, I had my first taste of kataifi. In the early morning hours after dancing, we would eat kataifi shreds rolled up like large shredded wheat, coated in honey, and topped with nuts.

Preheat the oven to 375°F.

Combine the butter and honey in a large saucepan and heat over medium-low heat, stirring just until the butter is melted. Whisk to combine and set aside.

Unfold the kataifi on a countertop. Grab one end of a bundle of strands about ½ inch thick with one hand and use your other hand to wrap the kataifi around the fingers (but not the thumb) of the hand holding the kataifi. When you have almost completely wrapped the kataifi around your fingers, twist the loose end into the nest to secure it and place on an ungreased baking sheet. Repeat with the remaining kataifi.

Bake 10 to 15 minutes, or until golden brown. Remove the nests from the oven and brush/dab them with the honey butter. Sprinkle each one with a few flakes of salt.

The nests will stay fresh at room temperature for up to 3 days.

Serve warm or cool with a scoop of Mango Lassi Frozen Yogurt (page 75), or another frozen yogurt or ice cream.

Makes 18 to 24 nests

½ pound (2 sticks) unsalted butter

1 cup honey

One 1-pound package frozen kataifi (shredded phyllo dough), thawed

Maldon sea salt

CAST-IRON PANCAKE

An eggy, puffy, not-too-sweet pancake made in a cast-iron pan.

I make this giant pancake at home regularly. It is the easiest thing to put together. It's delicious covered with a heavy snowfall of powdered sugar and some generous squeezes of fresh lemon juice. Or vary the recipe by throwing thin slices of apple or halved cherries into the bottom of the pan while it's heating up and then pouring the batter on top to bake.

In fact, I've even been known to use this very batter for savory versions. We'll fry up some thin-sliced bacon in a cast-iron skillet, leave the grease in the pan, and pour the batter right into the grease, then throw the chopped bacon into the batter. It can be breakfast, lunch, dinner, or dessert, depending on how you make it and what you serve it with. I love this with Huckleberry Frozen Yogurt (page 74) or Fresh Ginger Frozen Yogurt (page 76).

Makes 8 to 10 servings

4 tablespoons (½ stick) unsalted butter

4 large eggs, at room temperature

¾ cup unbleached all-purpose flour

¾ cup whole milk

Pinch of fine sea salt

3 tablespoons salted butter, melted

Powdered sugar

1 lemon

Preheat the oven to 425°F.

Put the unsalted butter in a 10-inch cast-iron skillet and place it in the oven to preheat the pan and melt the butter.

Meanwhile, beat the eggs in a bowl, then add the flour, milk, and salt and stir just to blend; the batter should still be lumpy.

When the oven is preheated, carefully remove the hot pan (using oven mitts) and pour in the batter. Immediately return the pan to the oven and bake for 20 minutes, or until the pancake is puffy and golden brown.

Remove from the oven and pour the melted salted butter on top. Sprinkle with the powdered sugar and some lemon zest (use a Microplane grater), and squeeze some lemon juice on top.

Slice, sprinkle with more powdered sugar, and serve immediately with ice cream or frozen yogurt.

THE STEPS

Everything into the bowl.

Dramatically puffy! Remove from the oven and drizzle melted butter all over.

Time for the first coating of powdered sugar.

Grate a bit of lemon zest over the top, then squeeze the juice. I like lots of lemon juice. The pancake will begin to deflate.

Slice into 8 to 10 pieces while still very hot.

Sprinkle with even more powdered sugar to taste. It will form a kind of crust. Yum.

PEORIA CORN FRITTERS

Fried soft corn fritters dunked in powdered sugar.

Corn fritters were a favorite treat when I was growing up in Illinois. Every fried chicken joint in Peoria had them, and we would bring buckets of them home to eat in our own kitchen or drive an hour and wait in line to get a table in a packed, smoke-filled bar with loud music, the best fried chicken ever, and powdered-sugar-coated corn fritters.

And you know what? They are delicious with ice cream, especially our Buttermilk Soft-Serve (page 68). They are really easy to pull together, and instead of corn, they can be made with equal amounts of fruit, chopped roughly into the same size as corn kernels, to make cherry fritters, apple fritters, peach fritters, and so on.

Fritters should be made just before serving, but the first batches can be kept warm in a 200°F oven until ready to serve. I throw the hot fritters right into the waiting bowl of powdered sugar so that the oil absorbs and melts the sugar and creates a sweet crust.

Heat the oil in a 4-quart saucepan over medium heat until it reaches 365°F.

Put the powdered sugar in a large bowl and set aside.

If using fresh ears of corn, slice the kernels from the cob, then "milk" the cob by scraping with the back of your knife to extract the liquid; reserve 1½ cups of the kernels and liquid. If using frozen corn, pulse the kernels in a food processor 10 times to break up the casings and let the juices out.

Break the eggs in a medium bowl and beat them with a fork until they are uniformly yellow. Add the milk and beat with the fork until incorporated. Add the flour and mix well, then add the corn and mix to blend.

When the oil has reached 365°F, or when a drop of batter sinks to the bottom and quickly floats up again with bubbles all around, drop 3 spoonfuls of batter into the oil, one at a time and evenly spaced.

Serves 8 to 10

5 cups vegetable oil, for deep-frying

2 cups powdered sugar

2 ears fresh corn, or 1½ cups thawed frozen corn

3 large eggs

1½ cups whole or 2% milk

2½ cups unbleached self-rising flour

Fry the fritters for 4 minutes, flip over, and fry another 4 minutes, until deep golden brown. Using a slotted spoon, remove from the oil, drain for a few seconds on paper towels, and dredge in the powdered sugar. Repeat until you've used up all the batter. Serve warm.

Ⓖ NORTH MARKET WAFFLES

Fluffy, airy, and yeasty, crisp on the outside, hot and soft inside: the best waffles in the world.

The busiest time in Columbus's North Market is Saturday morning, so for years, as we were building our reputation, we made these waffles to give folks a reason to come over. We would load them up with tastes of our ice cream while the waffles baked, and then they might add a pint to take home. Eventually we had long lines and half-hour waits. Trust me when I say that these are the *ultimate* American waffles.

The batter is put together the night before, and it gets really airy overnight. The results are fantastic: crispy outside, light and a bit chewy inside, with a warm, yeasty flavor. I love these for breakfast with our Sweet Cream Ice Cream with Blackberry Jam (page 28).

Makes 8 to 10 servings

2½ cups whole milk

½ pound (2 sticks) unsalted butter, cut into 16 pieces

3 cups unbleached all-purpose flour or gluten-free flour

1 cup whole wheat flour or gluten-free flour

2 tablespoons sugar

2 teaspoons fine sea salt

1 tablespoon instant yeast

4 large eggs, at room temperature

2 teaspoons vanilla extract

Heat the milk and butter in a small saucepan over medium-low heat until the butter melts. Let cool until warm to the touch, about 105° to 110°F (if it's hot on your finger, it's too hot).

Combine the flours, sugar, salt, and yeast in large bowl. Add the milk mixture and whisk until smooth. Whisk the eggs and vanilla in a small bowl until combined, then add to the batter and whisk until incorporated. Scrape down the sides of the bowl with a rubber spatula and stir until smooth. Cover the bowl with plastic wrap and refrigerate for at least 12 hours, and up to 24 hours.

Heat your waffle iron (always heed the manufacturer's instructions). Remove the waffle batter from the refrigerator. The batter will be deflated; whisk it to recombine.

Use about ½ cup batter per waffle in a 7-inch round iron or about 1 cup in a 9-by-9-inch iron. Bake the waffles for 4 minutes, or until golden but not brown, and not caramelized or toasted. Serve immediately, or keep warm in a single layer on a wire rack in a 200°F oven while you cook the remaining waffles.

SWEET EMPANADAS

Hot, sweet-tart fruit inside a crispy, nutty fried crust.

These can be made with almost any type of fruit and are superb, but the most sinful dessert in this whole book are these Sweet Empanadas stuffed with Corn Syrup Custard (page 183). Serve those, and you will become famous for them.

Although these are cute when hand-formed, we now use a sealer (see Sources, page 200), which gives us perfect empanadas every time, and is faster, too. Fry these up and serve hot out of the fryer. Put them in bowls, grab your ice cream scooper and roll some ice cream up in it, then use the ice-cream-loaded scooper to crush each pie right in its swollen center: the fruit will come out as the crust cracks and parts and the steam will melt part of the ice cream and turn it into sauce. Nothing else needed in that bowl but spoons.

Of course, you can eat these out of hand. And if you allow them to cool completely, you can dunk them whole in Sweet-Tart White Icing (page 192); let the icing dry before serving.

Makes 10 to 12 empanadas

DOUGH
3 cups unbleached all-purpose flour

3 tablespoons sugar

¾ teaspoon fine sea salt

½ cup high-quality lard or vegetable shortening

1 large egg, beaten

1 cup buttermilk

FILLING
1 pound apples, peaches, plums, or apricots, peeled, cored or pitted, and diced, or 1 pound blueberries, blackberries, or raspberries

½ cup sugar

¼ teaspoon fine sea salt

2 tablespoons lemon juice

1 teaspoon cornstarch

Vegetable oil for deep-frying

To make the dough, combine the flour, sugar, salt, and lard in a food processor and pulse 10 to 15 times until the mixture resembles coarse crumbs, with some larger flakes of lard strewn throughout. Add the beaten egg, stirring gently with a fork, then add the buttermilk and stir gently until it all comes together. Form the dough into a ball and wrap in plastic wrap. Refrigerate for at least 1 hour.

To make the filling, combine the fruit, sugar, salt, lemon juice, and cornstarch in a medium saucepan and cook over medium heat, stirring until the mixture has thickened slightly. Remove from the heat and allow to cool.

To assemble the empanadas, on a floured surface, roll the dough into a large rectangle about ⅛ inch thick. Use a 4- or 5-inch biscuit cutter to cut 10 to 12 circles from the sheet. Loosely gather any leftover scraps, knead tightly until the dough comes back together, roll out as before, and cut additional circles; repeat as needed.

Place 2 to 2½ tablespoons filling in the center of one round of dough. Fold the dough in half and crimp the edges to seal. Repeat with the remaining rounds and filling.

Heat the vegetable oil to 365°F in a large deep saucepan. Working in batches, fry the empanadas, turning once, for 2 to 4 minutes per side, until the dough is rich golden brown. Drain on paper towels and transfer to a plate in a warm oven while you cook the rest of the empanadas. Serve warm.

Chocolate Empanadas

A different filling can make the empanadas even sweeter! Instead of the fruit filling, make the Chocolate Glaze (page 189), using 2 tablespoons of milk to create a chocolate paste—you should have about 2 cups. Fill each empanada with about 2 tablespoons of this paste and continue as directed.

HOW TO MAKE EMPANADAS

Making empanadas is really easy, especially if you have an inexpensive little hand-pie mold. The process is fast, too. You can do many of these in no time if you follow these quick steps.

THE STEPS

Lightly flour the surface. Roll out the dough to ⅛ inch thick. Use the back of the mold to cut rounds (I use the 5- inch mold).

Gently press the dough into the open mold.

Place 2 tablespoons of filling right into the center; be careful not to get any on the sides, or the pie won't seal.

Fold the mold together, crimping the two sides as you press.

Combine any leftover scraps, roll it out again, and cut out additional rounds. Repeat as directed in previous steps.

This will all go very fast. In no time at all you're ready to fry 'em up!

VANILLA-BEAN ICE CREAM BREAD PUDDING

Best bread pudding ever: a soft, luxurious pudding served with Whiskey Caramel Sauce.

This started as a fun experiment, but turned out to be one of our favorite test kitchen desserts. The dish makes an easy case for buying a pint of well-made ice cream from your local grocer, melting it, and baking with it. A high-quality pint of ice cream like our Ndali Estate Vanilla Bean has lots of flavorful ingredients already in it, so you won't have to buy them. Plus, it's a good story to tell your guests—and this is such an easy recipe that you can memorize it and make it on the fly pretty much anywhere.

Makes 8 to 10 servings

3 cups brioche or challah (crusts removed) roughly torn into 1-inch pieces

4 large eggs, at room temperature

1 pint leftover vanilla ice cream, melted

¾ cup lukewarm water

1 cup sugar

Whiskey Caramel Sauce (page 187)

The recipe calls for brioche or challah, but you can use whatever you have. My friend Rusty Hamlin, chef for the Zac Brown Band, uses biscuits in his bread pudding. Anything goes, but remember that the heartier the bread and the harder the crust, the longer you need to let it sit in the melted ice cream mixture to soften before you bake it.

Serve scoops of it right from the oven, doused with the caramel sauce and garnished with sliced bananas, nuts, and whipped cream to make a "hot" ice cream sundae. How cool is that?

Preheat the oven to 350°F.

Place the brioche in a 9-by-13-inch baking dish. Beat the eggs in a large bowl. Add the melted ice cream, water, and sugar and mix well. Pour the mixture over the brioche and let sit for 15 minutes.

Bake for 35 minutes, or until the top looks caramelized. Remove from the oven, douse with the sauce, and serve warm.

BANANAS FOSTER

Bananas, dark brown sugar, brandy, and the possibility of flames.

The first time I made Bananas Foster, I thought I had died and gone to heaven. I began making it for demos when I was just starting out in the ice cream business. I decided to make Bananas Foster because it's quick and delicious. After watching my demo and having a taste, customers would walk over and buy one or two of our pints to serve with it when they made it at home.

Bananas Foster has a place in culinary history near Crepes Suzette, Caesar Salad, Châteaubriand, Cherries Jubilee, and all those other famous dishes prepared or finished tableside by a trained server in a crisp waiter's jacket.

If you are a showman, you can ignite this at the table, but that seems a little extreme to do at home, don't you think? You might want to invite your friends into the kitchen to watch you set it aflame when you add the alcohol. If it doesn't naturally ignite, you could use a stick lighter, but actually, I have never found that flambéing the sauce makes a difference in the flavor, so I choose to let it simmer a little bit after I add the brandy. Do be aware that when you add the alcohol you might see some flames—don't panic, they will die out quickly.

Spoon this over Salty Vanilla Frozen Custard or any other flavor you wish, and top with whipped cream if desired.

Makes 8 servings

4 tablespoons (½ stick) unsalted butter, softened

½ cup packed dark brown sugar

2 tablespoons banana liqueur (see Sources, page 200)

4 medium slightly underripe bananas, halved on the diameter and then halved lengthwise

½ cup brandy

Pinch of fine sea salt

Salty Vanilla Frozen Custard (page 60)

Melt the butter in a 10-inch heavy skillet over low heat. Add the brown sugar and stir until it is evenly moistened. Add the banana liqueur and bring to a simmer. Add the bananas and cook, turning once, for about 30 seconds on each side, carefully spooning sauce over the bananas as they cook. Use a large slotted spatula to remove the bananas and divide among eight bowls, leaving as much of the sauce in the pan as possible.

Bring the sauce to a simmer and carefully add the brandy. If the sauce is very hot, the alcohol will ignite and then burn out momentarily; if it does not, just allow it to simmer for 3 to 4 minutes, until the sauce thickens a bit and becomes syrupy. Add the salt and stir.

Spoon the hot sauce over the bananas and serve immediately alongside a scoop of the ice cream.

POACHED FRUIT

Poaching softens fruit and brings out its pure flavors.

Poached fruit is elegant. The fruit comes out of its hot wine-and-sugar bath all shiny and soft. You can serve the syrup with it too. Lay a poached peach or pear on top of a small scoop of ice cream—your spoon will sink easily into the fruit and catch some of the ice cream below in each bite.

Because poaching fruit brings out all its flavor, you don't have to start with perfect specimens. Some peaches and apricots have yellow flesh beneath a skin with gorgeous deep peachy-red spots. I really go for that, and I feel disappointed when I get a plain yellow one: the flavor might be very good, but the peaches look blah. So I take a raw beet, cut it in half, and dab the exposed side onto the peach to give it hot-pink cheeks. No one is the wiser, but it goes a long way to making your poached peaches pop on the plate!

Combine the wine, sugar, and spices or herbs, if using, in a 4-quart saucepan and heat to just under a boil over low heat, stirring to dissolve the sugar.

Gently place the prepared fruit into the warm poaching liquid and cook, turning the fruit in the liquid as needed, until it is tender.

Using a slotted spoon, gently remove the fruit from the poaching liquid and serve hot, or allow to cool on a plate. Once it has cooled, the fruit can be stored in an airtight container, covered with the poaching liquid, in the refrigerator for up to 3 days.

Makes 8 servings

1 bottle white or red wine,
  or 3 cups water

2 cups sugar

Spices or herbs as desired
  (I love star anise in winter,
  sweet basil in summer)

4 large pears or peaches, or 8 plums,
  peeled, halved, and pitted, or 16
  medium apricots, halved and pitted,
  or 50 cherries (about 1 pound), pitted

COOKING TIMES FOR POACHED FRUIT

Fruit	Amount	Time
Pears	4	15 minutes
Peaches	4	15 minutes
Plums	8	10 minutes
Apricots	16	5 minutes
Cherries	about 50	2 minutes

SAUTÉED FRUIT

Softened, slightly caramelized fruit with lots of juices.

When I don't have a lot of time to make dessert, I'll bring home some ice cream and sauté some fruit.

The method reads more like driving directions than a recipe. That's because there is more than one way to get there and sometimes you have to make adjustments on the fly, depending on what fruit is available and what wine you've got open.

To serve 4 people, budget about 1 large peach, nectarine, plum, pear, or apple (1 or 2 more if you are using smaller plums or nectarines), plus 1 cup fresh berries. You'll also need some butter, ½ cup wine (red or white), ½ cup sugar, and 1 pint ice cream. You can also add crumbles of cookies or gravel at the end if you'd like. To serve 8, double everything.

Slice the peach, nectarine, plum, pear, or apple into large slices. Drop 1 generous tablespoon of butter (salted or unsalted) into a 10-inch sauté pan over medium-high heat. When melted and hot, add the fruit slices. Cook for a few minutes on each side, until softened. (Harder fruit will require more time on the heat to soften and will caramelize more.) When the fruit is softened and beginning to caramelize, remove it from the pan. Add the sugar and cook with the juices, if any. Add the wine and simmer with the sugar to reduce just a bit. Remove from the heat and toss the sliced fruit back in, along with the berries, until just warmed through and glossy from the juices.

If you wish, add a grating of lemon zest, a squeeze of citrus, some turns of black pepper, or some fresh herbs before taking off the heat. Serve warm, over or under ice cream.

Makes 8 servings

2 tablespoons unsalted butter

2 pears, peeled, cored, and sliced (about 2 cups)

½ cup sugar

Splash of red or white wine

Pinch of fine sea salt

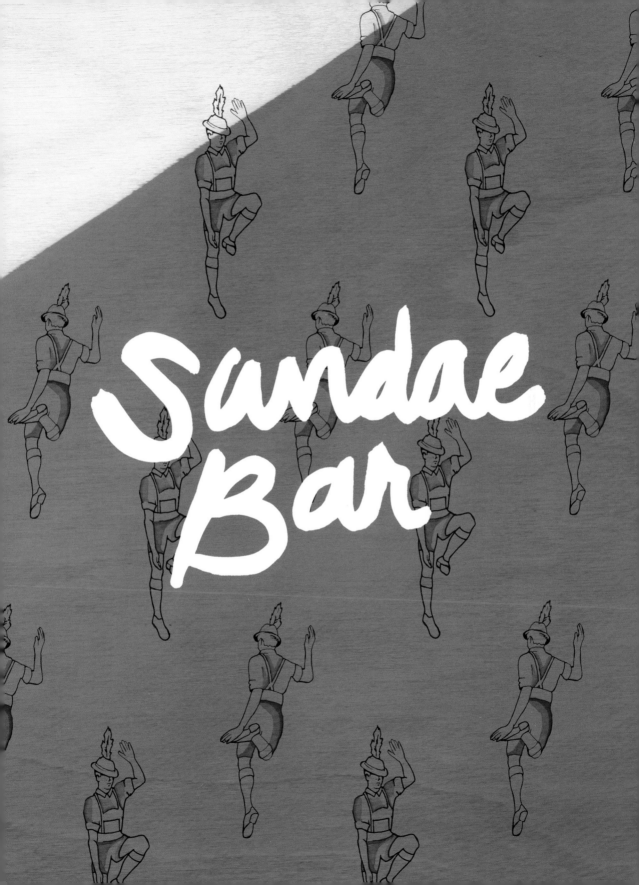

Sundaes, parfaits, big tall cakes, and cocktails—they always make the party, whether it's a casual get-together with friends, a holiday meal with your family, or a backyard shindig with the neighbors. This chapter includes many options for desserts and drinks to serve at parties of all stripes.

The recipes in this book are meant to be mixed and matched into a multitude of composed desserts (or uncomposed desserts).

You can build an impressive Ice Cream Layer Cake (pages 170–75) by fitting alternate layers of cake and ice cream into a silicone springform cake mold and topping it with whipped cream and garnishes. Ice cream cakes are spectacular in form and flavor. Countless cocktails can be concocted with varying combinations of ice cream, sorbet, and booze—the only limit is your own imagination, so jump in and belly up!

And so it goes for sundaes and parfaits. What's the difference between the two? Not much. I interchange them, depending on what sounds better in the name that I come up with for the dish. But my general rule is that a parfait is composed of two mini sundaes, usually stacked in a tall clear vessel to reveal all the layers. That said, I never follow rules religiously, not even my own rules. I don't feel bound by definitions and neither should

you. Still, most of the time if there is only one of each layer I'm calling it a sundae, unless, of course, the name sounds better as a parfait as in the Plum Sake Parfait (page 161), and then I throw all the rules out the window and just go with it.

And you know of course that any sundae, parfait, cake, or cocktail worth the time to make it ought to go out into the world with a name. Think of the traditional colorful names like Tin Roof or Nesselrode or Banana Split. At Jeni's, we have the One Night in Bangkok, the Chocomole, and The Salty Grahama (page 156). I love it when someone presents a dessert or cocktail with a fancy name to me, it ratchets up the whole situation.

Once you've sprinkled, layered, and drizzled your way through the chapter, use the original combinations as your springboard, and let your imagination soar. Mix and match sauces, gravels, ice creams to create your own cakes, cocktails, and parfaits, or create a sundae bar where guests assemble their own one-of-a-kind masterpieces.

THE EXIT THROUGH THE CAFÉ

A frozen strawberry cheesecake in a tall glass.

Whipped Cream (page 191)

Farmstead Cheese Ice Cream
(page 34), made without the jam

Salty Graham Gravel (page 195)

Macerated Strawberries
(page 184)

Mint

A SUNDAE IN SAN JUAN

This is a sundae I had from the drive-thru at
Church's Chicken in San Juan, Puerto Rico, in 1995.

Salty Vanilla Frozen Custard
  (page 60)

Fried Biscuits (page 123)

Macerated Strawberries (page 184)

Honey Whipped Cream
  (page 191)

Pineapple Sauce (page 184)

THE SALTY GRAHAMA

All it's missing is a string of pearls.

Whipped Cream
   (page 191)

Salty Vanilla Frozen
   Custard (page 60)

Sliced banana

Whiskey Caramel Sauce (page 187)

Salty Graham Gravel (page 195)

THE AUSTRIAN DANCING KICK

Pumpernickel with a kick in the lederhosen.

Whipped Cream
(page 191)

Dark Chocolate & Rye
Whiskey Ice Cream (page 40)

Pumpernickel Gravel
(page 196)

Whiskey Caramel Sauce
(page 187)

Mint

THOUSANDAIRE'S SUNDAE BRUNCH

Brunch in a bite: donuts, French toast, sweet cream, gold, caramel, and pecans.

THE KRISPY QUEEN

A powdered-sugar-coated fried biscuit donut sundae.

Whipped Cream (page 191)

Fried Biscuits (page 123)

Buttermilk Soft-Serve (page 68)

Donut Gravel (page 194)

Blackberry Jam (page 182)

Fresh blackberries for garnish

THE JENNIFER JUNIPER PARFAIT

Juniper ice cream, lemon curd, and blackberry-infused whipped cream.

Fresh blackberries for garnish
Whipped Cream (page 191)
Blackberry Jam (page 182)
Lemon Curd (page 183)
Juniper Ice Cream (page 39)

PLUM SAKE PARFAIT

An understated sophisticated dessert.

Sugared Croutons (page 193)

Honey Whipped Cream (page 191)

Sliced plums

Plum Sake Sorbet (page 87)

THE KEY LIME PARFAIT

All the components of a key lime pie, and a little more.

1 fresh cherry for garnish

Whipped Cream (page 191)

Chocolate Gravel (page 196)

Lime Curd (page 183)

Graham Cracker Ice Cream
  (page 46)

BERRY BISCUIT CAKES

Buttery, salty, soft, and flavorful Bauer House Biscuits
make a magical strawberry shortcake.

Bauer House Biscuits (page 122)
Macerated Strawberries (page 184)
Sweet Cream Ice Cream (page 28)
Honey Whipped Cream (page 191)

PÊCHE MELBA

A legendary sundae, easy to assemble, bright and beautiful.

Salty Graham Gravel (page 195)

Poached Peach half (page 148)

Salty Vanilla Frozen Custard
   (page 60) or Sweet Cream Ice
   Cream (page 28)

Fresh Red Raspberry Sauce
   (page 185)

CRÈME SANS LAIT SUNDAES ⓥ

Two killer, modern sundaes for any boy or girl.

Hi Boy

Mint

Sliced banana

Brrrr Sauce (page 186)

Banilla Crème sans Lait (page 71)

Atta Girl

Mint

Macerated Strawberries (page 184)

Rose Water & Pistachio
   Crème sans Lait (page 71)

J-BARS

Ice cream, sauce, and nuts on a stick, generously dipped in a bittersweet chocolate outer shell.

I call these delicious treats J-Bars because my name is Jeni, but if your name is Mary you can call them M-Bars and if your name is Ivan, you can call them I-Bars.

Making J-Bars is a multistep process, but it is well worth the effort. The chocolate shells are thicker than those found in the freezer aisle and the ice cream is dense and creamy. I like to pair Salty Caramel Sauce and Sweet Cream Ice Cream with smoked almonds. You can make all sorts of ice cream "candy bars" on a stick. Or leave out the sticks and then you have a frozen candy bar to end all candy bars.

The nuts can be left whole or chopped—whichever you like best.

Line a baking sheet with wax paper and place it in the freezer. Put the caramel sauce in a squeeze bottle and refrigerate.

Fill two 5-bar silicone ice cream molds (see Sources, page 200) with the ice cream and level the tops with an offset spatula. Insert a stick into each mold. Cover with wax paper and freeze for 30 minutes, just to slightly firm up the ice cream.

Using the handle of a small spoon, scrape out a small trench in the center of each mold and fill the trench with caramel sauce. Press 3 to 5 bits of the nuts into the ice cream in each mold. Cover the molds with wax paper and return to the freezer to fully harden, 3 to 4 hours.

Combine the chocolate and coconut oil in a double boiler and heat over medium heat, stirring, until all the chocolate is melted and the coconut oil is fully incorporated. Remove from the heat, transfer to a small deep bowl, and allow to cool until still fluid but not hot.

Remove the J-Bars from the freezer and pop each one out of the mold. Dip each bar by the stick into the chocolate and count to 3, then remove it, allowing the excess chocolate to drip back into the bowl of chocolate, and set the bar on your prepared baking sheet. Return the J-Bars to the freezer to harden for at least 2 hours.

Makes 10 J-Bars

½ cup Salty Caramel Sauce (page 187)

Sweet Cream Ice Cream (page 28), or 1 quart ice cream of your choice, slightly softened

½ cup smoked, toasted, or salted nuts, such as almonds, pecans, or peanuts

12 ounces bittersweet chocolate (at least 60% cacao), chopped

⅓ cup refined coconut oil

ETON MESS PLATTER

Meringues, softly whipped cream, ice cream, sorbet, and berries arranged in an artful mess.

The Eton Mess is a classic dessert that traces its origins to Eton College, the Hogwarts-like British boarding school. It is traditionally made with strawberries, broken meringues, and cream. We make ours with macerated berries of all varieties, ice cream and/or sorbet, crushed meringues (handmade or store-bought), and piles of softly whipped cream.

What I love about this dessert is that you can assemble it on a large platter with two large serving spoons and let your guests decide what and how much to serve themselves. This is particularly fun after a dinner served the same way, like a platter of pasta or a roasted chicken and vegetables.

To assemble, place alternating scoops of Sweet Cream Ice Cream and Red Raspberry Sorbet—or any flavors you wish—on a large platter. Break some meringues up and scatter the pieces over the top; too many is about enough here. Then spoon the macerated fruit over it all and add loose clouds of whipped cream. Grate some very fine lemon zest and toss it and some pretty mint on top. Gather a stack of small dessert plates and a handful of spoons and take it all to the table.

Eton College may have many great traditions, but I see no reason not to break every rule with an Eton Mess—it's yours to create.

Red Raspberry Sorbet (page 88) and Sweet Cream Ice Cream (page 28)

2 Meringue Cake disks (page 102), crumbled

Macerated Strawberries (page 184), plus other berries

Honey Whipped Cream (page 191)

Mint

ICE CREAM LAYER CAKES

My cakes, molded with layers of cake, sauce, and ice cream, are more like terrines. The top is decorated simply with a layer of whipped cream (added right before slicing) and fruits, nuts, or gravel.

While I switch flavors, sauces, and garnishes constantly, the layers are always the same. And they always begin with either Lady Cake (page 100) or A Wiseman's Chocolate Cake (page 98) and we build from there. As with sundaes, parfaits, and cocktails, you can choose whichever components you wish—the combinations are infinite!

ASSEMBLING AN
ICE CREAM LAYER CAKE

You'll need one 9-inch silicone springform pan; 1 Lady Cake (page 100) or A Wiseman's Chocolate Cake (page 98); 2 pints of ice cream (one recipe from this book); ⅔ cup of a sauce; Whipped Cream (page 191); and your choice of garnishes for topping the cake right before you serve.

Cut the cake in half horizontally.

Fit the first layer of the cake into the bottom of the silicone pan (cut side facing up) and spread on ⅓ cup of sauce, if using.

Spread a softened pint of ice cream, yogurt, frozen custard, or sorbet evenly over the sauce.

Add the second half of the cake (cut side facing down) and, if desired, another ⅓ cup of sauce.

Spread another pint of softened ice cream over the sauce.

Be sure the last layer is smooth and flat. Put the cake in the freezer for at least 6 hours to harden.

Just before serving, whip some cream and remove the cake from the freezer.

Spread the sweetened whipped cream on top of the cake.

Top with fresh fruit, crushed meringues, more sauce, gravel, nuts, or any accoutrement you want.

THE LITTLE HAVANA CAKE

Lady Cake, Guava Jam, Double-Toasted Coconut Ice Cream,
and Cajeta, topped with meringues and whipped cream.

1 Lady Cake (page 100)

⅔ cup Guava Jam (page 182)

⅔ cup Cajeta (page 187)

Double-Toasted Coconut
  Ice Cream (page 42), made
  without cajeta

About 1 cup Whipped
  Cream (page 191; made
  just before serving)

Meringues, for crushing just
  before serving

BIG BLACKBERRY BUTTE

Tart Huckleberry Frozen Yogurt, Blackberry Jam,
Lady Cake, and a sprinkling of fresh blueberries and mint.

1 Lady Cake (page 100)

⅔ cup Blackberry Jam (page 182)

Huckleberry Frozen Yogurt
  (page 74)

About 1 cup Whipped Cream (page
  191; made just before serving)

Fresh blueberries, huckleberries,
  or blackberries for topping the
  cake just before serving

Fresh mint

SKUNK AS A DRUNK CAKE

Black and white and whiskey all over.

1 A Wiseman's Chocolate Cake
(page 98)

1 cup Whiskey Caramel Sauce
(page 187)

Sweet Cream Ice Cream (page 28)

About 1 cup Whipped Cream (page
191; made just before serving)

1 cup Rosemary Bar Nuts (page 192)

COCOA ROCOCO

Four different chocolates kick up the luxe factor.

1 A Wiseman's Chocolate Cake
(page 98)

⅔ cup Runny Chocolate Sauce
(page 190)

1 cup Chocolate Gravel (page 196),
for topping the cake just before
serving

Salty Goat's-Milk Chocolate
Frozen Custard (page 60)

About 1 cup Whipped Cream
(page 191; made just
before serving)

COCKTAILS

If you consider the many ice creams and sorbets in this book, and the array of spirits in the world today, you can begin to imagine the possibilities for ice cream cocktails. A sorbet is the perfect mixer and ice in one—pulverized fruit, juices, and sugar, all frozen together—and a shot of liquor over a scoop of sorbet is all you need for a killer cocktail. As milk cocktails—spirited drinks made with milk and cream and liquors—make a comeback in bars across America, keep in mind that ice cream makes an amazing milk cocktail.

Host a cocktail and dessert party in one. You can riff on the classic cocktail, and even make it better, as in my rendition of the Salty Dog, which I call the Salty Bitch (photograph below): it's phenomenal. You can also create brand-new ones such as the Sword in the Stone (photograph on facing page) to serve as your signature cocktail!

SALTY BITCH

My favorite cocktail of all time. Charly's too.

Makes 1 drink

Murray River Sea Salt or Himalayan coarse pink sea salt
  (see Sources, page 200)
One 4-ounce scoop (about ¼ pint) Grapefruit Sorbet
  (page 85)
¼ cup vodka
Sprig of tarragon

Pour a thin layer of the salt onto a small plate. Moisten
the rim of a lowball glass and gently dip into the salt to
coat. Drop the scoop of sorbet into the glass and pour
the vodka over the top. Garnish with the tarragon sprig
and serve with a spoon.

SWORD IN THE STONE

*A sword lodged in a moss-covered stone,
surrounded by spirits and juniper trees,
awaiting Arthur.*

Makes 1 drink

¼ cup gin
2 tablespoons pear liqueur
One 4-ounce scoop (about ¼ pint) Wheatgrass,
  Pear, & Vinho Verde Sorbet (page 91)
1 cocktail sword

Shake the gin and pear liqueur with ice in a shaker to
chill. Place the scoop of sorbet in a chilled Champagne
coupe or a martini glass (or kingly goblet) and plunge
the sword into it. Pour the gin mixture on top and serve.

ROUGE YOUR KNEES

**Red Raspberry Sorbet tastes grassy and
fresh in this juicy cocktail.**

Makes 1 drink

One 4-ounce chunk (about ¼ pint) Red Raspberry Sorbet
  (page 88)

¼ cup gin

1 to 2 ounces soda water

Twist of lime

Sprig of lavender

Lean the chunk of sorbet against the side of a tall
glass. Pour the gin over and add soda water to your
taste. Garnish with the lime twist and sprig of lavender.

LADY OF THE LAKE

Commemorating when the Lady of the Lake gave the sword Excalibur to King Arthur.

Makes 1 drink

¼ cup vodka or gin

2 tablespoons Sweet Cream Ice Cream (page 28) or Jeni's Ndali Estate Vanilla Bean Ice Cream

One 4-ounce scoop (about ¼ pint) Stone Fruit Sorbet (page 90)

1 cocktail sword

Shake the vodka and ice cream in a shaker until the ice cream is just melted and incorporated. Place the scoop of sorbet in a chilled Champagne coupe and plunge the sword into it. Pour the vodka all around it and serve.

THE BASICS

Here are the elemental recipes that you will use to build flavors of ice creams, cakes, sundaes, and other desserts in this book. These components are also handy when you are concocting your own flavors and desserts.

To shake things up, feel free to add other dry spices to the gravels, or liquor to the sauces. For example, our famous Salty Caramel Sauce (page 187), which we sell in jars at Jeni's, is a versatile taking-off point. It can be made into Ancho-Orange Caramel Sauce by adding pinches of ancho chilies and orange zest (it's perfect on the Stone-Ground-Grits Pudding Cake, page 106). The same base can also mutate into Miso Caramel Sauce, Whiskey Caramel Sauce, or Goldschläger Caramel Sauce with one twist or another on the ingredients. I'm sure you'll have your own ideas and use these recipes as inspiration for all those wonderful yet-to-be-created dishes!

BLACKBERRY JAM

Tart-sweet deep purple jam.

Swirl this jam into ice cream or whipped cream
(page 191), or spread it between split Bauer House
Biscuits (page 122). Spread ½ cup in the center of
Lady Cake (page 100).

Makes about 1¼ cups

2 cups fresh or frozen blackberries

1 cup sugar

Combine the berries and sugar in a 1-quart saucepan,
bring to a boil over medium heat, and stir to dissolve
the sugar. Continue boiling, stirring occasionally for
8 minutes. Let cool slightly, then force through a sieve
if you want to remove the seeds.

Refrigerate until cool, at least 2 hours.

The jam can be stored in the refrigerator for up
to 2 weeks.

GUAVA JAM

**An easy-to-make dense guava jam, with a very
pretty color and lovely floral scent.**

This jam is tailor-made for a cheese course or swirling
into Farmstead Cheese & Guava Jam Ice Cream
(page 34).

Makes about 1½ cups

3 to 4 guavas

2 tablespoons fresh lemon juice

1 cup sugar

Cut the guavas in half and remove the pulp; measure
out 1 cup for the jam. Puree the pulp with the lemon
juice in a blender until smooth. Strain out the seeds
and reserve the liquid.

Combine the sugar and guava liquid in a small
saucepan and cook, stirring occasionally, for 5 minutes,
until it thickens slightly. Remove from the heat and
let cool.

The jam can be stored in the refrigerator for up to
2 weeks.

MANGO JAM

**A fantastic bright yellow-orange sweet fruit jam
that punctuates any ice cream with color and a
burst of exotic flavor.**

Makes about 1 cup

2 ripe mangoes, peeled, pitted, and cut into ½-inch pieces

⅔ cup sugar

1 tablespoon fresh lemon juice

Puree the mangoes in a food processor until smooth.

Combine the mango puree, sugar, and lemon juice
in a medium saucepan, bring to a boil over medium
heat, and cook for 5 minutes, stirring to dissolve the
sugar. Let cool to room temperature, about 2 hours.

The jam can be stored in the refrigerator for up to
2 weeks.

PEACH JAM

Make when peaches are delicious and freeze to relive summer later in the year.

Use this jam to make Cream Biscuits with Peach Jam Ice Cream (page 36) or top biscuits or cake with it.

Makes about 1½ cups

2 large peaches
¾ cup sugar
Juice of ½ lemon

Bring a large pot of water to a boil. Cut a small X in the bottom of each peach. Fill a large bowl with ice and water.

Blanch the peaches in the boiling water just until the skin begins to peel back at the X, 5 to 15 seconds. Transfer to the ice bath to cool; drain.

Peel the peaches, using a soft-skin peeler (see Sources, page 200). Slice the peaches in half from top to bottom and twist to separate the fruit from the pit. Puree the peaches and measure out 1 cup puree for the jam.

Combine the peach puree, sugar, and lemon juice in a medium saucepan, bring to a boil over medium-high heat, stirring to dissolve the sugar, and boil for 8 minutes, until it thickens slightly. Remove from the heat and let cool to room temperature, then refrigerate for up to 2 weeks.

CORN SYRUP CUSTARD

It's the goop around the pecans in a pecan pie. 'Nuff said.

This custard is the *jam*: it is spoon-right-into-your-mouth good. One of my favorite recipes in the whole book is our Sweet Empanadas (page 140) stuffed with Corn Syrup Custard, eaten out of hand or with a scoop of ice cream.

I created this recipe because the stuff around the pecans in a pecan pie is amazing. And you cannot make it without corn syrup.

Makes about 1 cup

3 large eggs, at room temperature
½ cup packed dark brown sugar or honey
½ cup light corn syrup
Pinch of fine sea salt
1½ teaspoons vanilla extract
¾ cup salted toasted pecan halves (optional)

Preheat the oven to 300°F.

Whisk the eggs in a large bowl until slightly frothy. Add the brown sugar, corn syrup, salt, and vanilla and whisk very well to combine. Add the pecans, if using, and stir to coat.

Pour the mixture into a 9-inch square baking dish. Bake for 30 to 35 minutes, rotating the dish halfway through, until the edges are set, but the center still jiggles slightly; do not overbake. Let cool completely on a rack, then refrigerate.

LEMON OR LIME CURD

For making ice cream parfaits, or swirling into ice cream.

We make this curd extra tart, the way I like it, and also because the lemon or lime juice will lose a little tartness when frozen. It's also made with more sugar than a traditional curd. This keeps it from becoming hard as a rock when frozen in ice cream. Although traditional lemon curd does not contain starch, I add tapioca starch or cornstarch to bind some of the water in the juice, so that if you swirl it into ice cream, it won't become juicy. We layer pockets of the lemon curd into our Juniper Ice Cream (page 39).

Makes 2 cups

4 large egg yolks

1 tablespoon tapioca starch, or cornstarch

¾ cup sugar

Grated zest of 1 lemon

¾ cup lemon juice

8 tablespoons (1 stick) unsalted butter, cut into
½-inch cubes

Put the yolks and the tapioca starch in a medium bowl and mix until completely smooth. Add the sugar, zest, and juice and blend well. Pour into a 4-quart saucepan and place over medium heat.

Stirring constantly, heat the mixture until it begins to simmer (7 to 10 minutes). Allow to simmer for 45 seconds. Remove from the heat and whisk in the butter, one cube at a time, until melted and smooth.

Pour the curd into a bowl and press plastic wrap onto the surface to prevent a skin from forming. Chill completely, about 2 hours, in the refrigerator. The curds will keep in the refrigerator for up to 2 weeks.

MACERATED STRAWBERRIES

Strawberries macerated in enough sugar to make them really juicy.

The sugar in these keeps the juice from freezing in ice cream. Use these with Bauer House Biscuits (page 122) and Sweet Cream Ice Cream (page 28) for a bang-up strawberry shortcake. Or on A Sundae in San Juan (page 155).

Makes about 1½ cups

1 pint strawberries, hulled and sliced

½ cup sugar

Toss the strawberries with the sugar in a large bowl. Let sit for 3 hours in the refrigerator.

PINEAPPLE SAUCE

For the Hummingbird Cake Ice Cream or banana splits.

Makes about 2 cups

1 cup fresh pineapple, finely chopped

½ cup pineapple juice

½ cup corn syrup

¾ cup sugar

Combine all of the ingredients in a 4-quart saucepan and bring to a boil over medium-high heat, then reduce the heat and simmer for 8 minutes. Remove from the heat and let chill.

The sauce can be stored in the refrigerator for up to 2 weeks.

FRESH RED RASPBERRY SAUCE

This uncooked red raspberry sauce is extra bright in color and flavor.

Makes about 1½ cups

One 12-ounce bag frozen raspberries or 1 pint fresh
½ cup sugar

Puree all ingredients in a blender. Pour into a small bowl, cover, and let sit in the refrigerator for at least 2 hours to allow the sugar to dissolve.

RED CURRANT–STRAWBERRY SAUCE

Bitter and pleasantly astringent from the red currants, a flavorful and colorful swirl for ice cream.

Makes about 2 cups

1 cup currants
1 cup strawberries
1 cup sugar

Puree the fruit in a food processor until smooth. Force through a sieve to remove the seeds.

Combine the puree and the sugar in a small saucepan, bring to a boil over medium-high heat, stirring to dissolve the sugar, and boil for 5 minutes, stirring. Let cool completely and refrigerate for up to 2 weeks.

RUM-PLUMPED PRUNES

Juicy and plump, rum prunes are like the Incredible Hulk of raisins.

Makes about 1 cup

¾ cup prunes, pitted
½ cup sugar
½ cup water
2 tablespoons rum (or Cognac)
2 tablespoons fresh lemon juice

Combine all the ingredients in a medium saucepan and bring to a boil, stirring to dissolve the sugar. Remove from the heat and let cool. These will keep in the refrigerator for up to 2 weeks.

Drain the fruit before using.

Variation Puree the prunes, adding a little of their juice until saucy, then use as a swirl in an ice cream.

STEWED RHUBARB SAUCE

Stewed rhubarb has a sweet-tart flavor and lovely pink color. A great contrast to ice cream or as a topping for a cake.

Rhubarb makes a bright, tart sauce that is perfect with ice cream or frozen yogurt, or on top of the Vanilla-Bean Ice Cream Bread Pudding (page 144). We also use it to fill the Sweet Empanadas (page 140). Look for rhubarb stalks with a lot of bright red and pink, or the sauce may turn grayish green.

Makes about 1½ cups

2 cups ½-inch chunks fresh or frozen rhubarb
½ cup sugar
1 tablespoon water

Combine the rhubarb, sugar, and water in a medium saucepan and bring to a boil over medium-high heat, then reduce the heat and simmer until the rhubarb is soft and falling apart, about 10 minutes. Serve warm beneath ice cream or cold on top.

The sauce keeps for up to 2 weeks in the refrigerator.

WHITE HOUSE CHERRIES

Fresh cherry flavor and color, with a burst of concentrated red cherry from the dried cherries.

We use this sauce for a blast of cherry flavor in desserts or mixed into ice creams. The dried cherries have a concentrated red cherry flavor, and the fresh cherries have a sparkly fresh flavor and texture. Or serve it as a topping for Farmstead Cheese & Guava Jam Ice Cream (page 34), with Salty Graham Gravel (page 195), if you want an excellent cheesecake sundae.

If you are making this to swirl into ice cream, you can halve the recipe. If you are using it to top ice cream, it will serve at least eight.

Makes about 2 cups

2 cups pitted fresh tart red cherries or frozen cherries
½ cup dried cherries
1 ½ cups sugar
⅔ cup water

Combine the cherries, sugar, and water in a 4-quart saucepan, bring to a boil over medium-high heat, stirring to dissolve the sugar, and boil for 5 minutes. Remove from the heat and allow to cool for 30 minutes.

If you will be mixing the cherries into ice cream, drain them or puree them, adding a little bit of the liquid to thin the sauce as needed.

Store in the refrigerator for up to 2 weeks.

Ⓓ Ⓥ Ⓖ BRRRR SAUCE

An incredibly tasty dairy-free sauce akin to the extravagant French butter caramel sauces.

It's nice to have a complete vegan dessert at the ready as part of your go-to dinner party recipes, just in case you need it. Brrrr Sauce also makes a nice fondue with mangoes, apples, peaches, cubes of cake, and a dash of whiskey stirred in. Yep.

Earth Balance is a vegan "buttery spread," and I'm not gonna lie, "buttery spread" hurts my ears. But there is no denying its rich butteriness. It makes this decadent sauce taste like it's straight out of a confectioner's shop in Breton. Hard to believe it doesn't contain a drop of cream.

Do not double this recipe. When you use the dry-burn technique, as I do here, you want the sugar to just coat the bottom of the pan. If you put too much sugar in, it won't melt evenly and it will turn into clumps that are hard to dissolve. But it comes together very quickly—if you want to double the amount, just make two batches.

Makes about 1 cup

¾ cup sugar
⅔ cups rice milk or almond milk
1 teaspoon vanilla extract
6 tablespoons Earth Balance Buttery Spread, softened
Pinch of fine sea salt

Sprinkle the sugar evenly over the bottom of a heavy-bottomed 4-quart saucepan and set it over medium-high heat, standing by with a heatproof spatula. Do not touch it until a ring of melted darkening sugar surrounds the unmelted white sugar in the center; then use the spatula to pull the hot melted sugar into the unmelted sugar. Continue to push the sugar together and stir until it is all melted and evenly medium amber in color.

Remove from the heat. Using caution, add the rice milk a little at a time and stir until incorporated. If you get any lumps of hardened sugar, place over medium heat and stir until completely melted.

Add the vanilla and buttery spread and stir until well combined. Add the salt. Serve immediately, or store in the refrigerator for up to 1 week. The sauce will separate as it cools; just heat it and stir again.

CAJETA

A sauce of rich, complex caramelized goat's milk.

I first had dulce de leche in Puerto Rico sometime in the mid-1990s, and I immediately began making ice cream with it. Cajeta is a Mexican version, made with goat's milk. It's great to swirl into or drizzle over ice cream.

Makes about 2 cups

6 cups goat's milk
1 cup packed dark brown sugar
¼ teaspoon baking soda

Combine the milk, brown sugar, and baking soda in a 4-quart saucepan and bring to a boil over medium-high heat, whisking to dissolve the sugar. Reduce the heat to a heavy simmer and cook for 2 hours, stirring every 10 to 15 minutes, or until the sauce has thickened and is a rich caramel color.

The sauce will keep in the refrigerator for up to 2 weeks.

SALTY CARAMEL SAUCE

A beautiful caramel sauce with a nutty aroma.

This sauce is made for drenching the Vanilla-Bean Ice Cream Bread Pudding (page 144), or for rolling down a mountain of ice cream. The color of the caramelized sugar will determine the depth of flavor in the sauce. I sometimes like paler amber caramels, and sometimes richer red-brown ones. Sugar loses sweetness if it burns, though, so don't let it go too far. You can use rum or brandy or any spirit you want to make this sauce; apple cider is also nice, or just leave the spirits out.

Do not double this recipe. If you need twice the amount, make it twice instead.

Makes about 1 cup

⅔ cup sugar
¾ cup heavy cream
Big pinch of fine sea salt

Sprinkle the sugar evenly over the bottom of a heavy-bottomed 4-quart saucepan and set it over medium-high heat, standing by with a heatproof spatula. When you see that there is a layer of melted sugar underneath the unmelted white sugar in the center of the pan, use the spatula to mush and stir the hot melted sugar into the unmelted sugar. Continue to push the sugar together until it is all melted and evenly medium amber in color. Remove from the heat. Using caution, slowly add the cream a little at a time, stirring constantly until incorporated. If you get any lumps of hardened sugar, place on medium heat and stir until completely melted.

Pour the sauce into a bowl and let cool slightly, then stir in the salt.

Whiskey Caramel Sauce As you stir in the salt, add 2 tablespoons of your favorite whiskey.

Ancho-Orange Caramel Sauce As you stir in the salt, add 1½ teaspoons ground ancho chili and 1 teaspoon superfine orange zest.

Miso Caramel Sauce As you stir in the salt, add 2 tablespoons of white miso paste.

Goldschläger Caramel Sauce As you stir in the salt, add 2 tablespoons of Goldschläger.

Roasted Garlic Caramel Sauce You will not believe how tasty this is on ice cream! Wrap a whole head of garlic in foil and roast in a 400°F oven for 35 minutes, until caramelized and smoky. Squeeze the roasted garlic from its husk and stir it into the caramel sauce with the salt.

HOT HONEY

Honey spiked with loads of cayenne.

We get our honey from Val Jorgensen, who is also our mint grower. She makes hot honey from her hives, and it's great on ice cream.

You can also drizzle this on fried chicken, or make a mixture of half Hot Honey and half melted salted butter for a memorable corn bread glaze.

Makes 2 cups

1½ cups honey

½ cup water

1 to 2 teaspoons cayenne pepper, or to taste

Combine the honey, water, and cayenne in a small saucepan and heat over low heat for 10 minutes. Remove from the heat and let steep for 1 hour.

Pour the honey through a fine sieve, and use immediately or let cool. The honey keeps indefinitely at room temperature.

PINK PLUM PUCKERY SAUCE

Pulverized plum skins make this a bitter-sweet-tart, neon-pink accessory for plain frozen yogurt.

This sauce is great on a Pêche Melba (page 164) instead of the raspberry sauce. Or make an apricot Melba to go with it.

Makes about 2 cups

6 plums

1 cup sugar

1 cup fresh lemon juice (from 4 to 5 lemons)

Peel the plums with a soft-skin peeler (see Sources, page 200) or a paring knife, reserving the skins. Cut 4 of the peeled plums into ½-inch chunks. Reserve the other 2 peeled plums for another use—I recommend eating them now!

Combine the plum cubes, reserved skin, sugar, and lemon juice in a small saucepan and bring to a boil over medium heat, whisking to dissolve the sugar. Simmer for 8 minutes. Remove from the heat and, with caution, puree it in a blender. Force the sauce through a fine-mesh sieve into a bowl and let cool for 30 minutes.

Serve at room temperature.

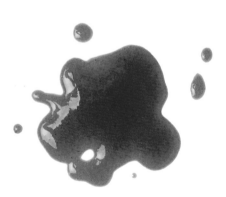

CHOCOLATE GLAZE

Shiny chocolate for drizzling, dunking, or spreading.

Made with just a splash of milk (2 tablespoons), this chocolate glaze is spreadable and can be used as a frosting or a filling stuffed into Sweet Empanadas (page 140).

With a tiny bit more milk, it becomes more fluid, so you can spread it or pipe it onto a cookie or other sweet treat. A little more milk, and you can pour it onto the top of a cake or Éclairs (page 130), but it will still sit up, not sink into the pastry. Add even more milk, and you have a drizzle—more than that, and you will have soup.

Makes about 2 cups

6 tablespoons (¾ stick) unsalted butter

3 ounces unsweetened chocolate (99% cacao), chopped

3 cups powdered sugar

2 to 6 tablespoons whole milk (see table)

Melt the butter and chocolate in a small heavy saucepan over low heat. Stir in the sugar, then slowly stir in the amount of milk to reach the desired consistency. Remove from the heat and use immediately.

HOW MUCH MILK TO USE FOR CHOCOLATE GLAZE

Use	Recipe	Amount
Chocolate paste	Chocolate Empanadas	2 tablespoons
Spread or pipe	Jake's Chocolate Truffle Cookies	3 tablespoons
Dip or pipe	Cream Puffs; Eclairs	4 tablespoons
Drizzle	Ring Cake	5 tablespoons
Soup	—	6 tablespoons

White Chocolate Glaze Substitute white chocolate for the unsweetened chocolate and then proceed as directed, while using the proper amount of milk to reach the desired consistency as per the table.

RUNNY CHOCOLATE SAUCE

A dark, bitter chocolate sauce for serving on top of ice cream or mixing into ice cream.

This complex, bittersweet sauce is fluid even when cold, meaning you don't have to heat it up to serve. And it makes fantastic hot cocoa or chocolate milk—just add milk until it's as light as you want it, then heat it. The better the chocolate, the more complex the flavor of the syrup.

Makes 2 cups

1½ cups water

¾ cup sugar

¾ cup Dutch-processed cocoa powder (99% cacao)

1 ounce unsweetened chocolate (99% cacao), finely chopped

Combine the water, sugar, and cocoa powder in a 2-quart saucepan, bring to a boil over medium-high heat, whisking to dissolve the cocoa and sugar. Boil for 30 seconds, then remove the pan from the heat, add the chocolate, and let stand for 5 minutes.

Whisk until the chocolate is fully melted, then process in a food processor until smooth and glossy, about 2 minutes. The sauce can be served hot or cold. It keeps for about 2 weeks in the refrigerator.

GOAT'S-MILK HOT FUDGE SAUCE

A very rich and creamy sauce that hardens when cold; condensed goat's milk gives it tanginess.

Use this to top or garnish a cake or ice cream. The goat's milk makes it more of a milk chocolate sauce, but it is still rich and dark.

Makes 2 cups

1 cup condensed goat's milk (or condensed cow's milk)

⅓ cup muscovado sugar (see Sources, page 200) or packed light brown sugar

½ cup light corn syrup

¼ cup Dutch-processed cocoa powder (99% cacao)

6 ounces unsweetened chocolate (99%), finely chopped

Combine the goat's milk, sugar, and corn syrup in a 2-quart saucepan and bring to a simmer over medium-high heat, stirring to dissolve the sugar. Remove from the heat, add the cocoa powder, and whisk until moistened. Return to the heat and whisk again until it comes to a boil. Remove from the heat, add the chocolate, and let sit for 5 minutes.

Stir the sauce until the chocolate is completely melted and smooth. Serve warm, or let cool and refrigerate. The sauce can be refrigerated for up to 2 weeks; reheat over gentle heat until fluid.

MARSHMALLOW FILLING

A bright white frosting that is especially great on A Wiseman's Chocolate Cake.

Makes about 2 cups

8 tablespoons (1 stick) unsalted butter, softened

½ cup marshmallow cream

1 pound powdered sugar

2 to 3 tablespoons whole milk

1 vanilla bean (seeds scraped out) or 1 teaspoon vanilla extract

Beat the butter and the marshmallow cream in a large bowl using a hand mixer on medium speed until well blended. Add one-third of the sugar, beating on low until well mixed and all sugar is incorporated; repeat with another third. Repeat with the rest of the sugar, beating until all is combined.

Add 2 tablespoons of the milk and the vanilla and continue beating on low speed until smooth. Increase the speed to high and beat for another 30 seconds until fluffy. Add a little more milk, just a dribble at a time, until you get the consistency you want. Use immediately or store in the refrigerator for up to 2 weeks; bring to room temperature before using.

WHIPPED CREAM

Making sweet, creamy, airy whipped cream is a fundamental skill for any ice cream maker.

We hand-whip all of our whipped cream in our shops. It is fast and easy, and it gives you more control over the texture. This recipe makes enough to serve 8 to 10 people a nice dollop.

If your dessert is very sweet, make your whipped cream less sweet. If your dessert is not so sweet, sweeten the cream a little more.

When I serve pie, I often whip the cream so that it is still runny and serve it over the pie.

You can also whip unsweetened cream to top warm soups like butternut or lobster bisque.

Makes about 3 cups

2 to 3 tablespoons sugar

1 teaspoon vanilla extract or brandy (optional)

1½ cups of heavy cream

Chill a large metal or glass bowl that is wider than it is tall (to make it easier to get full strokes and incorporate air into the cream) in the refrigerator for at least 15 minutes; it should be cold to the touch.

Pour 2 tablespoons sugar into the bowl. Add the vanilla or brandy, if using. Pour in a splash of cream and whisk until well blended, then add the rest of the cream and tilt the bowl so that the cream and sugar rest in the crook of the bowl. As you whip, imagine that you are pulling air into the cream. You do not have to go quickly, so don't overexert yourself. Just continually pull air into the cream in a round motion that begins at your elbow. You will create soft peaks in 2 to 4 minutes. If the cream doesn't taste sweet enough, add up to 1 more tablespoon sugar.

Honey Whipped Cream Honey gives the cream a floral and earthy sweetness without the cotton-candy sweetness of granulated sugar. Substitute honey for the sugar and omit the vanilla extract.

SWEET-TART WHITE ICING

A tangy icing for pies, cookies, or whatever you like.

It's fun to decorate the Sheet Pie (page 108) or Piekies (page 114) by flinging loose swirls or piping words of icing over the top crust—and it adds pops of sweetness to each bite. But if you want it to be more of a drizzle or a dip, use up to 4 tablespoons lemon juice. The thinner the icing is, the more it will get absorbed into a cake, which can also be very nice. You can dip Bauer House Biscuits (page 122) into it or drizzle it on top of the Lady Cake (page 100). If you make the Lady Cake with cornstarch and soak it in a looser form of this icing, you have yourself a tart, irresistible cake that makes a good summer dessert.

When you make the icing, at first it will seem like too much sugar and not enough liquid, but just keep stirring: it will come together. You can also use milk or water, tea or coffee, cranberry or cherry juice concentrate, hibiscus-steeped lemon juice (heat lemon juice until boiling, add hibiscus flowers, steep, strain, and cool) or another flavorful juice to make the icing.

Makes about 1 cup

2 cups powdered sugar

2 to 4 tablespoons fresh lemon juice (from 1 to 2 lemons)

Combine the powdered sugar and 2 tablespoons lemon juice in a medium bowl and stir with a fork or spoon until smooth. If desired, add more lemon juice a tiny bit at a time, until the icing is the consistency you want it to be. Put in a small Ziploc bag, cut the tiniest corner off, and go to town. Alternatively, you can spread it or fling it at will. In any event, use immediately—this icing will not keep.

ROSEMARY BAR NUTS

A standard at fine cocktail bars: brown sugar, rosemary, cayenne, and nuts of all varieties.

Rosemary Bar Nuts make our Yazoo Sue Ice Cream (page 58), but they can also top sundaes or fill a little dish for a cocktail party. They are tasty and easy. You can use whatever herbs or spices you wish, depending on what's in season. In the winter, for instance, make them with warm spices such as cinnamon, cumin, and cayenne. If you want to use leafier herbs, such as cilantro, basil, or chives, sprinkle them over the cooled nuts—experiment here, and feel free to omit the rosemary.

Makes about 2 cups

2 large egg whites

3½ tablespoons light brown sugar

¼ teaspoon fine sea salt

⅛ teaspoon cayenne pepper

1 teaspoon chopped fresh rosemary

2¼ cups mixed raw unsalted nuts, such as pecans, cashews, smoked almonds, or Spanish peanuts

Preheat the oven to 325°F. Line a baking sheet with parchment.

Mix the egg whites, brown sugar, salt, cayenne, and rosemary into a thick paste in a large bowl. Add the nuts and stir and toss until fully coated. Spread the nuts evenly on the baking sheet and roast for 30 minutes, tossing every 10 minutes, until toasty and aromatic. Transfer to another baking sheet and let cool.

The nuts can be stored in an airtight container at room temperature for up to 1 week.

SUGARED CROUTONS

Toasted, sugared, buttery, and crisp roughly hewn croissant pieces.

When you do not have the disposition or the wherewithal to make a cake or a more complicated dessert, these sweet croutons are for you. Serve with ice cream and fruit or fruit sauce in footed bowls, and your guests will think you are #brills and take pictures for Instagram.

I like to use croissants because they are decadently laced with butter, but you can make these with any bread, and the results will still be magical. Serve them warm from the oven or let them cool.

Makes 8 to 10 servings

6 croissants or 1 loaf bread of your choice

8 tablespoons (1 stick) unsalted butter

¾ cup sugar

½ teaspoon ground cardamom

Preheat the oven to 350°F.

Tear the croissants into 1-inch chunks. Melt the butter in a large saucepan over medium heat. Add the sugar and cardamom, stirring to dissolve the sugar, then toss the croissant pieces in the mixture to coat. Remove from the heat.

Arrange the croissant pieces on a baking sheet, allowing any extra butter to drip back into the saucepan. Bake in the oven for 20 minutes, tossing halfway through, until the croutons are crispy. Serve warm on top of ice cream or let cool.

GRAVELS

Crunchy condiments to complement ice creams.

Gravels give your ice creams and sundaes crunchy character and flavor! They can be made in any flavor you can dream up. We serve several different kinds at a time in our scoop shops. Here are some of our favorites.

DONUT GRAVEL

Potato donuts are traditional in the Midwest. The potato chips in this recipe add that potato flavor as well as a subtle fried flavor that mimics those fluffy potato donuts perfectly.

Makes 2 cups

1 cup plus 2 tablespoons unbleached all-purpose flour

1 teaspoon cornstarch

1¼ cups powdered sugar

2 ounces crushed potato chips
  (from about 2 cups whole chips)

1 teaspoon fine sea salt

Pinch of ground cinnamon

4 teaspoons nonfat dried milk

6 tablespoons (¾ stick) unsalted butter, melted

¼ teaspoon mixed sprinkles

Preheat the oven to 225°F.

Combine the flour, cornstarch, 1 cup of the powdered sugar, crushed chips, salt, cinnamon, and dried milk in a small bowl. Add the melted butter and stir until large lumps have formed and all of the dry ingredients are moistened (the mixture should resemble a wet, mealy dough). Toss with the sprinkles, then pour onto a baking sheet and spread evenly.

Bake the crumbs for 15 minutes. Remove the pan from the oven and toss the crumbs with two bench scrapers or metal spatulas, then chop into ⅛- to ¼-inch pieces.

Bake for 15 to 20 more minutes, or until lightly golden. Let the gravel cool, then toss with the remaining ¼ cup powdered sugar.

EVERYTHING BAGEL GRAVEL

Makes 2 cups

3 tablespoons dried minced onion

1 tablespoon sesame seeds

1 teaspoon poppy seeds

¾ teaspoon garlic powder

⅛ teaspoon cayenne pepper

¾ cup unbleached all-purpose flour

1 teaspoon cornstarch

½ cup sugar

¼ teaspoon malted milk powder

5 tablespoons unsalted butter, melted

2 teaspoons kosher salt

Preheat the oven to 225°F.

Combine the dried onion, sesame seeds, poppy seeds, garlic powder, cayenne, flour, cornstarch, sugar, and malted milk powder in a small bowl.

Add the melted butter and stir until large lumps have formed and all of the dry ingredients are moistened (the mixture should resemble lumpy wet sand). Add the salt, mixing just enough to distribute it evenly. Pour onto a baking sheet and spread evenly.

Bake the crumbs for 15 minutes. Remove the pan from the oven and toss the crumbs with two bench scrapers or metal spatulas, then chop into ⅛- to ¼-inch pieces.

Bake for 10 more minutes, until fragrant and toasted all the way through. Remove from the oven and let cool completely.

HOT BENNE SEED GRAVEL

In the South, regular sesame seeds are called benne seeds. We toss them with honey and chili paste and add some black sesame seeds and almond flour for effect.

Makes 2 cups

6 tablespoons toasted benne (sesame) seeds

1 teaspoon black sesame seeds

5 tablespoons honey

2 teaspoons sambal (garlic-chili paste)

¼ cup plus 2 teaspoons cornstarch

1½ teaspoons fine sea salt

1 cup almond flour

Preheat the oven to 225°F.

Combine the benne seeds, black sesame seeds, honey, chili paste, cornstarch, salt, and almond flour in a small bowl and stir until the mixture is combined and starting to flake apart into smaller crumbs. Pour the crumbs onto a baking sheet and spread evenly.

Bake the crumbs for 25 minutes. Remove the pan from the oven and toss the crumbs with two bench scrapers or metal spatulas, then chop into ⅛- to ¼-inch pieces. Bake for 25 more minutes, until toasted and fragrant. Remove from the oven and let cool completely.

SALTY GRAHAM GRAVEL

Makes 2 cups

1 cup finely ground graham crackers (from about 13 crackers)

¾ cup unbleached all-purpose flour

2 teaspoons cornstarch

½ cup sugar

2 teaspoons fine sea salt

8 tablespoons (1 stick) unsalted butter, melted

Preheat the oven to 275°F.

Combine the graham cracker crumbs, flour, cornstarch, sugar, and salt in a small bowl. Add the butter and stir until large lumps have formed and all of the dry ingredients are moistened (the mixture should resemble lumpy wet sand). Add the salt, mixing just enough to distribute it evenly. Pour the crumbs onto a baking sheet and spread evenly.

Bake the crumbs for 10 minutes. Remove the pan from the oven and toss the crumbs with two bench scrapers or metal spatulas, then chop into ⅛- to ¼-inch pieces.

Bake for 10 more minutes, or until gravel is a rich brown. Remove from the oven and let cool completely.

CHOCOLATE GRAVEL

Makes 2 cups

4 tablespoons (½ stick) unsalted butter

2 ounces unsweetened chocolate (99% cacao), coarsely chopped

1½ ounces bittersweet chocolate (64% cacao), coarsely chopped

¼ cup sugar

¼ cup packed light brown sugar

2 tablespoons unbleached all-purpose flour

1 tablespoon almond flour

1 tablespoon unsweetened cocoa powder

Pinch of fine sea salt

1 large egg

1 large egg yolk

1 tablespoon brewed coffee, cooled

1½ teaspoons molasses

¾ tablespoon vanilla extract

1 tablespoon heavy cream

Preheat the oven to 350°F. Butter a 9-by-13-inch baking dish.

Melt the butter and chocolates in a medium saucepan over medium-low heat, stirring until smooth. Transfer to a medium bowl and let cool slightly.

Add the sugar, brown sugar, flour, almond flour, cocoa powder, and salt to the chocolate mixture and mix until thoroughly combined.

Whisk together the egg, yolk, coffee, molasses, vanilla, and cream in another bowl until thoroughly combined. Add to the chocolate mixture and whisk just until combined. Pour into the prepared baking dish.

Bake for 25 to 30 minutes, or until a thin knife comes out moist; it will not be perfectly clean, but it shouldn't be sticky.

Let the chocolate loaf cool for 15 minutes in the pan.

Run a knife around the edges, invert it onto a wire rack, and let cool completely.

Preheat the oven to 300°F. Cut the loaf into 2-inch squares. Crumble them into ½-inch pieces. Spread evenly on two baking sheets and bake for 45 minutes, tossing every 15 minutes, until the pieces appear dried but not burned. Let cool completely.

PUMPERNICKEL GRAVEL

Makes 2 cups

3 cups coarsely ground pumpernickel bread (from 10 to 12 slices)

2 teaspoons caraway seeds

2 tablespoons ground caraway

2 teaspoons cornstarch

½ cup sugar

1 teaspoon fine sea salt

⅓ cup unbleached all-purpose flour

8 tablespoons (1 stick) unsalted butter, melted

Preheat the oven to 275°F.

Combine all the dry ingredients in a medium bowl and toss with the butter until the bread crumbs are evenly moistened. Pour onto a baking sheet and spread evenly.

Bake for 40 minutes, tossing the crumbs with a bench scraper or spatula every 10 minutes. Remove from the oven and let cool completely.

FRENCH TOAST GRAVEL

Makes 2 cups

6 ounces (1½ cups) toasted whole pecans

12 ounces brioche, challah, or white bread

⅓ cup unbleached all-purpose flour

4 teaspoons cornstarch

½ cup packed dark brown sugar

1 tablespoon fine sea salt

3 tablespoons nonfat dried milk

½ teaspoon ground cinnamon, plus 1 tablespoon

¼ teaspoon grated nutmeg

¼ teaspoon finely ground coffee beans

1 teaspoon vanilla extract

¼ cup maple syrup

4 large egg yolks

4 tablespoons (½ stick) unsalted butter, melted

1 cup powdered sugar

Preheat the oven to 300°F.

Finely chop 1 cup of the pecans. Set aside.

Combine the bread and the remaining ½ cup pecans in a food processor and process until all of the bread is reduced to crumbs and the pecans are pulverized. Transfer to a medium bowl, add the chopped pecans, flour, cornstarch, sugar, salt, dried milk, ½ teaspoon of the cinnamon, the nutmeg, and coffee, mix until well blended.

Combine the vanilla, maple syrup, and egg yolks in a small bowl and mix well. Add to the dry ingredients and toss until the bread crumbs are evenly moistened. Add the melted butter and toss well.

Pour the crumbs onto a baking sheet and spread evenly. Bake for 1 hour, tossing every 15 minutes.

Combine the powdered sugar and the remaining 1 tablespoon cinnamon in a medium bowl. Add the warm gravel and toss to thoroughly coat. Pour back onto the baking sheet and let cool completely.

HONEY CORN BREAD GRAVEL

Makes 2 cups

1 cup unbleached all-purpose flour

½ cup yellow cornmeal

¼ cup buttermilk powder

½ cup freeze-dried corn

⅓ cup sugar

2 teaspoons fine sea salt

5 tablespoons unsalted butter, melted

½ cup honey

Preheat the oven to 275°F.

Combine the flour, cornmeal, buttermilk powder, freeze-dried corn, sugar, and salt in a medium bowl. Add the butter and honey, stirring until large lumps have formed and all of the dry ingredients are evenly moistened (the mixture should resemble lumpy wet sand). Pour onto a baking sheet and spread evenly.

Bake 40 minutes, tossing every 10 minutes, until deep golden brown. Remove the pan from the oven, toss the crumbs with two bench scrapers or metal spatulas, then chop into ⅛- to ¼-inch pieces.

Bake for 10 more minutes, or until lightly golden. Remove from the oven and let cool completely.

THIS IS HOW WE DO IT

Jeni's Splendid Ice Creams is a community of craftspeople, winemakers, farmers, apiarists, cheese makers, artists, writers, musicians, big-brain thinkers, bikers, eaters, drinkers, travelers, and mathletes, all doing their part of the equation.

At our headquarters in Columbus, Ohio, we have Company Lunch once a month. It's a tradition that we have had for more than a decade. It all started in my home, where I would make dinner for our four or five employees every couple of months or so. We would all sit down together around my large dining room table (which now lives in our office as a meeting table). Today more than a hundred and fifty people show up regularly for Company Lunch.

At these lunches, we talk, share, conspire, and *eat*. Sometimes really cool things come out of the lunches, like the idea of engaging the extraordinary talents of our team to write and record an original album (Jeni's Company Band's holiday album, *Flavors from Earth,* is available on Spotify and iTunes and in vinyl at www.jenis.com).

To pull it off, our busy kitchens take a break from making ice creams to cook for the occasion. It's a nice change of pace for everyone and we go the extra mile to make it a not-to-be-missed event for our team. Why? Because when we all get together, we learn from and inspire one another, and we remember that #TeamJenis is bigger than just one person. We have raised this thing together.

It's easy to think that creative genius happens in a vacuum or at a lonely drafting table somewhere. But the truth is, creativity comes from people—lots of people, with lots of big or small ideas and thoughts. If you need inspiration, surround yourself with great people and listen to them.

Still, the ideas are just the beginning. Once you have one worth pursuing, the real work begins. You've got to try it, tweak it, try it again, push forward. And you've got to seek out those with expertise who can help you. Because not only do we need help finding ideas, we need help executing them. Lots of it.

I love the word "Company." It means that you are not alone, you are a part of a community. A good way to build a community is to feed people. A good meal with a memorable dessert is the perfect way to draw people together. This book is an extension of the Jeni's community, and in it, I have shared recipes that have become staples at Company Lunch. When it comes to dessert, ice cream is, of course, always our *numero uno*, but what we serve with it is just as important. We like to keep it simple, with the focus on the ice cream, because that's the most dynamic part of any dessert—the way it melts and changes while you eat it puts the whole thing in motion, adds urgency, and brings you into the moment—with your peeps.

At Jeni's, we have a shoot-for-the-moon attitude—because it's fun. We did not set out to just make a better ice cream than the next guy— that would be too easy. We set out to make the best ice creams that we could imagine. And there is always room to improve, which is all part of the gig. It means that we are always hungry, always in search of the next idea. That's what makes it all exciting. And we still have a way to go!

SOURCES

ALCOHOLS

Absinthe, Pernod, and pastis; banana and pear liqueur; Jonesy old tawny port; kirsch (cherry liqueur): well-stocked liquor stores.

White whiskey and stone fruit vodka: Middle West Spirits (www.middlewestspirits.com)

Plum sake: Sake One (www.sakeone.com/moonstone)

Yazoo Sue Smoked Porter: Yazoo Brewery (www.yazoobrew.com)

NATURAL EXTRACTS, SPICES, ESSENTIAL OILS, FLAVORINGS, AND COLORINGS

Almond extract (and many other extracts): Frontier Natural Products Co-op (www.frontiercoop.com)

Beet powder and beta-carotene: See Smell Taste (www.seesmelltaste.com) or Frontier Natural Products Co-op (www.frontiercoop.com)

Essential oils: Aftelier Perfumes (www.aftelier.com)

Natural butter flavoring (and many other natural flavorings): Frontier Natural Products Co-op (www.frontiercoop.com)

Matcha powder: Asian specialty food stores

Orange flower water: Mediterranean and Indian groceries

Sprecher's root beer concentrate: Midwest Supplier's (www.midwestsupplies.com)

Vanilla beans: Penzeys Spices (www.penzeys.com) or Whole Foods Market (www.wholefoodsmarket.com)

CHEESES

Cloverton Cheese: Laurel Valley Creamery (www.laurelvalleycreamery.com)

Follow Your Heart "Cream Cheese": Follow Your Heart (www.followyourheart.com) and many supermarkets

OTHER INGREDIENTS

Amarena cherries: Fabbri North America, available online and at many grocery stores

Annie's Honey Bunny Graham Crackers: Annie's (www.annies.com) and many grocery stores

Bob's Red Mill brand cake flour: Bob's Red Mill (www.bobsredmill.com) and many grocery stores

Chocolate, cocoas, and cocoa nibs: Askinosie (www.askinosie.com)

Gluten-free flour: Available at cup4cup.com

Evaporated goat's milk: Meyer's brand, available at Whole Foods Market and other grocery stores

Freeze-dried corn: Available at most groceries, including Whole Foods Market, and online at www.nuts.com

Huckleberries: Northwest Wild Foods (www.nwwildfoods.com)

Murray River Sea Salt: some specialty markets

Muscovado sugar: India Tree (www.indiatree.com) and natural food stores

Sweetened mango pulp: SWAD Kesar Mango Pulp from Patel Bros. Grocery Stores (www.patelbrothersusa.com)

EQUIPMENT

Hand sealer and silicone ice cream molds: available at www.amazon.com

Silicone springform pan: Nopro's Silicone Springform Pan with Glass Base (item #3939), available www.norpro.com or www.amazon.com

Skin-peeler: Zyllis's Serrated Soft Skin Peeler, available at kitchen supply stores and at www.zyliss.com

ACKNOWLEDGMENTS

During the past year—in addition to creating new flavors for Jeni's Splendid Ice Creams, along with the requisite lovely art campaigns and shop decor that accompanies those flavors—my small team and I wrote, tested, ate, photographed, and art-directed the book in your hands. It's been exhilarating, it's been exhausting, it's been delicious.

Making a book is a little like making a movie, I suppose. It takes a small village of experts to help pull it off, and with that in mind, roll the credits.

John Lowe, my friend and Jeni's CEO, kicked this whole thing off with his usual brand of levelheaded business dealings.

My trusted assistant, Matthew Troillett, managed the many details of this book and shared his fine, honest opinions at every turn (while juggling all of our other, non-book-related projects).

Kelsey McClellan, the extraordinary talent behind the camera lens, proved she's a one-woman show.

Pete Wiseman and Jacob Freisthler exemplified incredible stamina in the test kitchen with their understanding of the cycle that never stops: making, remaking, making, remaking, making, remaking. . . .

Aaron Beck uncovered countless errors, added humor, and otherwise carefully edited these pages.

My darling friend Michelle Maguire displayed her talent as a keen, eagle-eyed prop hunter, bringing character and life to photos of the desserts. And my pal Sally MacLeod did the irresistible illustrations for this book, including the peach butts, which she nailed.

Our in-house designers, Patrick Moore and Blake Roberts, offered insight, opinions, and special touches every step of the way.

Michael Moraine, my longtime friend and the new creative director of Jeni's Splendid Ice Creams, hustled to adjust every detail just in the nick of time.

Ryan Morgan, Chelsea Clements, and Lisa Steward—our social media team—help us make new friends near and far and spread the word about all we do here at Jeni's, including all things book-related.

The village of Jeni's, which is more than 500 strong and includes our growers, producers, kitchen team, shops teams, delivery teams, and creative and management alike, battles every day to make the best ice creams in the world and to do some good in the communities we serve.

The creative and technical know-how required to publish a cookbook is extraordinary. Artisan has it in spades, and I am honored to be on their list. Ann Bramson, my editor and Artisan's publisher, is a legend, with an acute understanding of readers near and far. Executive Managing Editor Trent Duffy moved us to get it done with an inspiring, rare blend of sternness and nurturing. Recipe editor Judith Sutton asked all the right questions to make everything both accurate and readable. Michelle Ishay expertly and elegantly fit everything we wanted between the covers of this book. Others on the Artisan team who made stupendous contributions are Renata Di Biase, Bridget Heiking, Cristina Krumsick, Allison McGeehon, Nancy Murray, Barbara Peragine, and Kara Strubel.

Special thanks go to my agent Jonah Straus—the best in the business!

I can always rely on my mother, Jacki, and my sister, Julie, to offer thoughtful, honest feedback. Finally, to my husband, Charly, and our minis, Greta and Dashiell—you have my heart.

INDEX

ABOUT THE AUTHOR

Jeni Britton Bauer has honed her ice-cream-making skills over nearly two decades and is the author of the *New York Times* best-selling *Jeni's Splendid Ice Creams at Home*. Dubbed the "homemade-ice-cream-making Bible" by *The Wall Street Journal*, her first book earned Jeni a James Beard Award, America's most coveted honor for those writing about food and the culinary arts.

The first Jeni's Splendid Ice Creams opened in 2002, in Columbus's North Market. There are now fifteen Jeni's scoop shops, from Chicago to Atlanta. Jeni's pints and ice cream sandwiches are also available at more than one thousand American groceries, as well as through Jeni's home-shipping business. Jeni's ice creams have been praised by *Time* ("America's best"), *Cooking Light* ("deadly delicious"), and *Saveur* ("revolutionary"), while *Food & Wine* said, "No one makes ice cream like Jeni Britton Bauer."

Today Jeni and her hands-on crew make every batch of ice cream, sorbet, and frozen yogurt in their kitchens in Columbus. They use cream from Ohio cows; Ohio honey; and whole fruits, vegetables, and herbs from nearby farms, as well as carefully sourced ingredients from around the world, including rare fair-trade vanilla (Uganda's Ndali Estate) and bean-to-bar chocolate (Missouri's Askinosie Chocolate).

When Jeni isn't developing new flavors or art-directing new campaigns, she devotes time to Local Matters (the fresh-food-for-all nonprofit she cofounded in Columbus), serves on the boards of the Wexner Center for the Arts and Columbus College of Art & Design, and gets into trouble with her husband and two children at their home in Columbus.

BIRTHDAY CAKE

What would an ice cream dessert book be without a killer birthday cake? You know these cakes are champions at sponging up that melting scoop of ice cream.

2 Lady Cakes (page 100) or
    A Wiseman's Chocolate Cake
    (page 98)

2 batches of Chocolate Glaze
    (page 196) or Marshmallow Filling
    (page 191)

Beeswax candles (optional)